# In Search of Piero

Attilio Brilli

# In Search of Piero

## A Guide to the Tuscany of Piero della Francesca

Electa

*Credits*
Biblioteca Comunale, San Sepolcro
National Gallery, Londra
Scala, Firenze
Soprintendenza B.A.A.A.S., Firenze e Arezzo
Tavanti, Arezzo


*Translation*
Deborah Hodges

Comitato nazionale per il Quinto Centenario
della morte di Piero della Francesca


Regione Toscana

Provincia di Arezzo
Comune di Arezzo
Comune di Monterchi
Comune di Sansepolcro
Comunità montana Valtiberina toscana

# Contents

# A Pilgrimage to Piero

*What Apelles could excell Pietro de Burgo for perspective, Albrecht Durer for drapery, Michelangelo for action".*

Henry Peacham, 1634

Piero della Francesca is a unique rather than unusual case of a great renaissance artist, who remained resident in his native village throughout his life, and whose most important works are still to be found today within a small and well defined area.

The route taken by either the modern traveller or the straightforward tourist in search of Piero della Francesca may coincide exactly with that taken by Piero himself during his travels as an apprentice, student and artist. The road, which led from Florence, the very centre of Tuscan civilization, to Borgo San Sepolcro, the small town situated on the borders of Umbria, Romagnia and Le Marche, represented for many years one of the main connections between dominions and principalities; as such it has been described with authority many times. To take this route, therefore, signifies following in the footsteps of the great painter, viewing the same landscapes and prospects, focusing in on the same perspectives of hills and valleys, discovering the unique integrity and artistic importance of the towns and countryside. As well as discovering his world, it signifies likewise discovering the stages in this artist's development, the creation and crystallization in form and colour of an art singularly lacking in eloquence, "with no urgent communication to make" – as Berenson wrote – "and no thought of rousing us with look or gesture". This is perhaps the reason why it has lasted so well in time.

Yet the incomparable and atmospheric nature of such an excursion lies in its development in time as well as space, in the present as well as in the past. This is made possible if the modern tourist adopts the same ancient route taken by famous travellers of the past; from the essayist and diplomat Montaigne, the geographer Furttenbach, and the historian Dennistoun to the poet W.B. Yeats, from Aldous Huxley

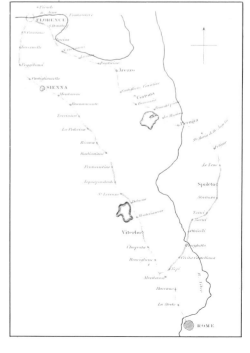

*Piero della Francesca, Resurrection, detail,*
*San Sepolcro, Civic Museum.*

*Piero della Francesca, Madonna del parto,*
*detail, Monterchi, Cemetery Chapel.*

to Albert Camus. He can see exactly what they saw and enjoy those experiences, which they knew how to describe to us.
From Florence to the upper valley of the Tiber, the itinerary in search of Piero della Francesca still conjures up a strong sense of discovery, of civilized and creative exploration. Not many years ago, the famous art historian, Sir Kenneth Clark, was able to note, with reference to the *Madonna del Parto*, that "it is one of the few great works of art which are still relatively inaccessible, and to visit it offers some of the pleasures of a pilgrimage."
A pilgrimage to Piero could be the alternative name for this secluded, silent and meandering itinerary, which seems unaware, at least in its last stretch, of the peremptory short-cuts of the modern road. It has the capacity, however, of revealing to us en route exceptional masterpieces, such as the frescoed cycle of the *Legend of the True Cross* in Arezzo, the *Madonna del Parto* in Monterchi, the *Madonna della Misericordia* and the *Resurrection* in San Sepolcro. In each case, these great masterpieces are to be found in, indeed are projected against, a background of the most humble, and often unknown, artistic works.
An inscrutable detachment gives the figures of Piero the mysterious, fixed quality of idols. With the fresh intuition of art and with careful calculation, these have never been detached from the roots of archaic wisdom, of primaeval posture. For this reason, their relatively recent re-evaluation in the wake of artists once described as "primitive" renders the evocative and sacred inspiration of a real pilgrimage even more plausible and significant.
The immediate and lasting fascination of this route for the modern traveller is increased by its unequalled reserve, its reluctance to disclose itself to the observer, to reveal the changing design of art and history in the forms of its landscape. Once again, the route towards Arezzo, Monterchi, Anghiari and from there, to the upper valley of the Tiber and San Sepolcro – the "borgo" of Piero – proves to be a journey in time and place; to the extent that the words of Edward Hutton used in 1905 to

Piero della Francesca, Madonna della Misericordia, detail, San Sepolcro, Civic Museum.

describe the objective of our journey, do not sound peregrine in our ears, but seem to indicate the most fabulous itinerary: "You journey over the mountains from Arezzo for hours amid all the clear beauty of Tuscan hills that have something not Tuscan about them and at last in the valley of the Tiber you come upon a tiny city at the foot of Monte Maggiore of the Central Appennines."

That city, no longer so tiny, is our destination; it is the final goal of our journey, which is also intended as a homage to one of the most disturbing works in the tradition of Western art, the *Resurrection* by Piero della Francesca – "the best picture in the world" – as Aldous Huxley described it – capable of revealing to us the renaissance of the classical and christian ideal in the figure of Christ, the guardian spirit of the town. Around San Sepolcro, destination of our pilgrimage, the landscape is so steeped in whispers and echoes of Piero that some years ago Leslie Gardiner was moved to write: " The river was thrown like a necklace round the mills and ruined abbeys and those hump-backed, fortress-crowned hills which had strayed out of the green forest. Those were my recollections, but perhaps I have confused personal memories with the Tiber that Piero della Francesca depicted..."

Is it still possible to allow oneself to be consciously seduced by a similar mirage, to discover the landscape of the upper Tiber through the art of Piero? For this to happen, and to have a more complete reconstruction of the area, we must first consider several works painted by Piero for San Sepolcro but no longer there; works which emphasize the close link between the artist and his native city. The *Baptism of Christ* and the *Nativity* in the National Gallery of London, and the *St. Jerome with a donor* in the Galleria dell'Academia of Venice reveal views of the city of San Sepolcro, and of the valley of the upper Tiber; exemplary representations of an ideal, classical microcosm, metaphor for the greater world, which in its own name and in the painting of its native artist recalls the words of an ancient local chronicler: "And our land of Borgo San Sepolcro was called

the New Jerusalem". A place which, by antonomasia, is the destination of every pilgrimage.

Only the knowledge of its own ironic and reflective nature can give the modern traveller a taste for an activity, suspended between discovery and invention, tactics and adventure. Every journey will then appear as a game of simulation with another type of journey which is not ours, with the comforts and discomforts to which we are not accustomed, in another age, which is not our own. Our companions, guides and teachers on this journey will be famous travellers, who have covered our route in differing epochs. Through their voices, near or far, harsh or soothing, the outlines of an environmental reality will take form before our disenchanted eyes; a reality both familiar yet strange, recognizable and yet unimaginable. Just as the traveller from the past would take with him topographical artists commissioned to paint the views enjoyed, the contemporary reader or traveller may illustrate his own journey with the work of those excellent

*Votive panel with a view of San Sepolcro, San Sepolcro, Civic Museum.*

12

*Piero della Francesca, Baptism of Christ,*
*London, National Gallery.*

*Piero della Francesca, St. Jerome with a
Donor, Venice, Galleria dell'Accademia.*

*Santi di Tito, Piero della Francesca,*
*San Sepolcro, Civic Museum.*

*Piero della Francesca, Nativity, London,*
*National Gallery.*

watercolour artists and those sophisticated engravers. By means of their work, he may double his direct, actual vision, and observe with their eyes. The journey in search of Piero will therefore coincide with the routes of many who promoted the discovery of this remote area, or merely described it. It is a method of travelling in time as well as space, in the imagination as well as in reality, without forgetting that an integral part of the fascination of the discovery of Piero and his land lies in the words of those travellers and fervent admirers of his work from every century and nation, from Montaigne and Dennistoun to the anonymous author of the guide to a pilgrimage to Loreto through Tuscan cities. Since a guide should aim not only at describing the actual route but also promote other, and more organic, literature, it is opportune to point out that certain works on Piero – Longhi's volume is one such example – are of a high literary standard and very enjoyable to read.

*"The active art-Lombardic... the contemplative art-Byzantine... Central stood Etruscan Florence-her root in the earth..."*

John Ruskin

"...there in the middle of the room were two sparkling jewels undimmed by time and varnish, Piero della Francesca's portraits of the Duke and Duchess of Urbino. In those days the Piero boom had not begun. I remember that, when Mr. Macdonald pulled out of his desk some sepia coloured photographs of the frescoes at Arezzo, I had immediately felt a sense of pre-ordained harmony different from anything that I had known. Piero's *Baptism* had given me more intense aesthetic delight than any picture in the National Gallery; but nothing had prepared me for the

brilliance and sparkle of the Urbino diptych". Following Clark's example, our journey in search of Piero begins with the Urbino diptych: the portraits of Federico da Montefeltro and his wife, Battista Sforza, with the scenes of the allegorical triumphs of the two sitters on the reverse sides. This mature work by Piero, painted at the court of the Montefeltro di Urbino and today in the Uffizi Gallery, also invites us to trace our steps back from the very middle of Piero della Francesca's life to the origins of his artistic development.

*The Early Florentine Renaissance*
It was in Florence that Piero's artistic initiation took place. Even though he had studied Sienese art on his commercial travels to that city and had been influenced by the genuine masterpieces in and around his native city, such as the polyptych with the Resurrection by Niccolò di Segna, the almost contemporary altar-piece of S.

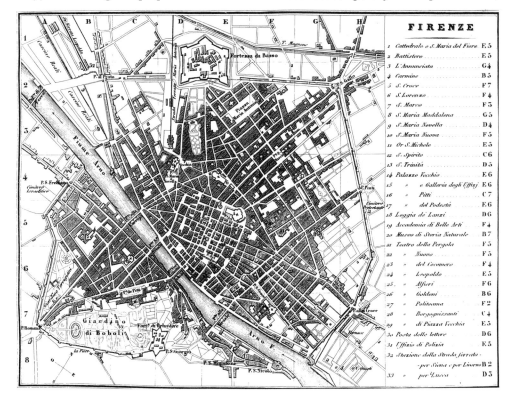

*J. Hakewill, View of Florence from S. Miniato, engraving.*

*J. Hakewill, View of Florence from Fiesole, engraving.*

*Joseph Pennell, View of Florence with the Arno, illustration for The Road in Tuscany, by M. Hewlett, London, 1904.*

*J. Pennell, View of Florence from S. Miniato, illustration for The Road in Tuscany, by M. Hewlett, London, 1904.*

Francesco by Sassetta in San Sepolcro and the similar polyptych with the Madonna and Child by Pietro Lorenzetti in Santa Maria della Pieve in Arezzo, he must have noticed the subtle signs of an inexorable decline. On the contrary, the city of Florence in the years immediately preceding 1439 – the year in which Piero is documented as working with Domenico Veneziano on the lost frescoes of Sant'Egidio – represented a kind of umbelical cord with the outside world for a young, talented man from a cultured, yet contested, province. In Florence, Piero was able to absorb the various elements of a very rich artistic tradition: from the lightness and delicacy of the late Gothic, provided by Masolino da Panicale, to the majestic temporality and grave narrative gestures of Masaccio; from the chromatic luminosity of Veneziano to the spatial science of Brunelleschi and Paolo Uccello; from the tormented, twisted figures of Andrea del Castagno to the secure, serene formality of Angelico. The entire city seemed to dedicate itself to the development of this young genius with his own sense of universality, of synthesis between humanism and christianity, with an appreciation of proportions, with a love of scientific rules. Clark observes that "the mathematics he learnt he absorbed partly through the brain and partly through the senses; partly through the teachings of Toscanelli, partly through the vaults and arcades of the Innocenti and the Pazzi Chapel. The *lucida ordo*, the belief in divine proportion, took root in his spirit during these early years, and was to expand there for the rest of his life".

But since this is only a guide with the aim of travelling in space as well as time, let us leave the Florentine artistic and cultural scene in the first half of the fifteenth century; we will return there whenever the memory of Florence – its science, its treatises and its art – re-appears in the painting of Piero della Francesca. After his youthful apprenticeship, Piero was never again to return to Florence to stay.

*Florence, or The View*

In Piero's day and almost to the end of the eighteenth century, Florence was first re-

J. Pennell, S. Miniato, 1904.

J. Pennell, Via Tornabuoni, 1904.

J. Pennell, Porta S. Frediano, 1904.

J. Pennell, Via Tornabuoni, 1904.

*J. Pennell, View of the Cathedral and Giotto's Bell-Tower, 1904.*

*J. Pennell, View of Piazza della Signoria, 1904.*

*J. Pennell, Il Bargello, 1904.*

*J. Pennell, View of Ponte Vecchio, 1904.*

*J. Pennell, On Ponte Vecchio, 1904.*

*J. Pennell, A Corner of Ponte Vecchio, 1904.*

vealed to the traveller approaching from Arezzo at a place suitably called l'Apparita (The Apparition). The Anglo-Florentine, W.B. Spence, lover of the Tuscan city and author of a delightful guide, describes it thus: "Opposite Maiano on the left is a high mountain surmounted by a convent called l'Incontro, and beyond, on the road to Arezzo, l'Apparita, 5 miles distant from Florence, celebrated as the place where the beautiful valley of the Arno and the distant city of Florence first burst on the view of the traveller who comes from Rome".

Florence is one of the rare cities of which mention of the view does not simply constitute an empty rhetorical phrase but still has some meaning. This is confirmed by the very recent travel notes of Julien Gracq, with their effective descriptions and eloquent comparisons : "The vision of Florence, caught in a flash as one turns the corner, astounds: from one side of the valley to the other, the horizontal level of the red roofs of the city completely fills the valley like a lake. Only here and there, the church towers and the dome of the cathedral break its surface. Nowhere do the city's suburbs spread up the sides of the hills, and this determines the real beauty of its hillside gardens, where one can look down, as though on the edge of a deep, still, silent pool. In Rome, the valley is more humped and the ring around it chipped and irregular; it lacks this exact and geometric horizontal line of roofs, which makes one think of the sedimented plateaux of a dry *chott*. Paris, seen from le Sacre Coeur, the maternal river-bed has long been flooded, the original layer of the city, altered and lost to the eye by the little hills, is no longer that of an enclosed lake: its stability is that of a gigantic sailing boat which spans two or three breakers at the same time."

Arriving in l'Apparita, it must have seemed to the young Piero that Florence and its valley transmitted the regests of an era. We are able to reconstruct its general aspect by means of the brief, but fresh and lively, notes of an illustrious English traveller at the end of the sixteenth century: "It is a most sweet City, and abounding

*J. Pennell, Tower in Via delle Oche, 1904.*

*G. Zocchi, The Uffizi Gallery.*

with wealth, the Citizens are much commended for their curtesie, modesty, gravity, purity of language, and many virtues. The City is innobled with the Dukes Court, and with stately Pallaces, built within and without the wals, and for the stately buildings and sweet situation, it is worthily called Florence the beautifull, vulgarly Fiorenza la bella......The River Arno running from East to West divides the Citie, but into unequall parts, the farre greater part lying on the North-side, and the lesse on the South-side; and the bridge to passe from one to the other, is almost in the very middest of the City, which is fairely built, yet is more magnified by strangers then it deserves. It hath little houses upon it, wherewith it is covered, and upon each side are Gold-smithes shops, which make small or no shew at ordinarie times: but when the Duke Ferdinando brought his Duchess (the Daughter of the Duke of Loraine) to the Citie, at her enterance, those shops were furnished with vessels of silver, and many rich Jewels, yet borrowed of the Citizens to that purpose."

*Echoes of foreign travellers*
Our English traveller also provides us with some amusing information concerning the reception offered by a budding Florentine tourist trade, explaining that Italian cities offered many houses, in which travellers could hire rooms, called "camere locanti"; in Florence, there were three or four, all in the same street and similar to those establishments called "hotels". Here one could hire a room for ten *giulii* a month, and the host had the duty to provide meals and sleeping quarters. He himself stayed in the hotel called 'Alle Chiavi d'Oro' in the house of Messer Bevigliano.

Today the longstanding and glorious establishment of Florentine tourism offers quite different "rooms with a view" from those taken by Moryson, Montaigne, or any of the other travellers from the distant past, who, notwithstanding the wonderful views, could not help but bemoan the lack of glass in the windows: "The windows are lined with paper, for the most part ripped, or falling apart, and are a disgrace to the beautiful stone houses". It is outside, how-

Piero della Francesca, Federico da Montefeltro,
Florence, Uffizi.

*Piero della Francesca, Battista Sforza,*
*Florence, Uffizi.*

*Piero della Francesca, The Triumph of
Federico da Montefeltro, Florence, Uffizi.*

*Piero della Francesca, The Triumph of Battista Sforza, Florence, Uffizi.*

QVE MODVM REBVS TENVIT SECVNDIS ·
CONIVGIS MAGNI DECORATA RERVM ·
LAVDE GESTARVM VOLITAT PER ORA ·
CVNCTA VIRORVM

28 ever, in the streets, the piazze and the palaces that Florence revealed, and still reveals, its true love of moderation, which forms an integral part of the spirit of the place. For a complete picture of Florence, observed from street-level, so to speak, and not from a panoramic viewpoint, we turn to Henry James, who was the visitor most sensitive to the environmental atmosphere. His unmistakeable chromatic notes remain imprinted indelibly on the mind of each observer. His extraordinary portrait, formed of scattered and fleeting notes, stands apart from the common rhetoric, and is one of the most enchanting homages ever paid to Florence. It still helps us today – notwithstanding everything – to glimpse at least a reflection of the true face of this "yellow" city: " All this brightness and yellowness was a perpetual delight; it was a part of that indefinably charming colour which Florence always seems to wear as you look up and down at it from the river, and from the bridges and quays. This is a kind of grave radiance – a harmony of high tints – which I scarce know how to describe. There are yellow walls and green blinds and red roofs, there are intervals of brilliant brown and natural-looking blue; but the picture is not spotty nor gaudy, thanks to the distribution of the colors in large and comfortable masses, and to the washing-over of the scene by some happy softness of sunshine. The river-front of Florence is in short a delightful composition. Part of its charm comes of course from the generous aspect of those high-based Tuscan palaces which a renewal of acquaintance with them has again commended to me as the most dignified dwellings in the world…. The great blocks of the basement; the great intervals, horizontally and vertically, from window to window (telling the height and breadth of the rooms within); the armorial shield hung forward at one of the angles; the wide-brimmed roof, overshadowing the narrow street; the rich old browns and yellows of the walls: these definite elements put themselves together with admirable art."

*Piero and the Diptych of the Duke and Duchess of Urbino*
The moment has come, however, to piece together our itinerary and direct our steps to the rooms of the Uffizi Gallery, which impressed Clark so greatly. Here Florence conserves its one and only work by Piero della Francesca. Due to its position in this city, so admired and visited by foreign travellers, the *diptych of the Duke and Duchess of Urbino* was already appreciated when a large part of the artist's work was still neglected. For example, the young American collector, Dan Fellows Platt, noticed in 1908: "Of Piero's works, I love best his Triumphs on the reverse of the Montefeltro portraits in the Uffizi. Do we see anywhere else so idyllic a landscape? – a broad plain, with dear little brown hills scattered all over it and the placid river winding in between; not to mention the little tufted trees with which the landscape is so regularly dotted."
The difficulty perhaps encountered by our visitor is no different from that of a reader who finds himself projected into the middle of a story, "in medias res", as Horace writes – in the middle of events – without having any idea of preceding developments. In the same way, our visitor finds himself in the presence of a mature work, in which Piero already communicates in that characteristically complex, high-flown, celebrative, yet realistic, language. The diptych can be given a psychological interpretation, such as that of the refined traveller of the twenties, André Suarès: "Everyone knows the portraits of the Duke of Urbino and the good Duchess, Battista Sforza, his wife, painted by Piero della Francesca. These are in Florence, but you can find them everywhere in Urbino. The Duke has a wide face, heavy and squared, and a great round head entrenched between his shoulders; an enormous neck; a great nose cut clean at its base, but round and powerful at its tip; a thin mouth with a mischievous curve which tempers somewhat the seriousness of the expression: this man likes to laugh, but not in a raucous way; he is simple and sincere, with a perfect dignity conscious of his position, without arrogance and with-

*Domenico Veneziano, Altar panel of S. Maria dei Magnoli, Florence, Uffizi.*

out familiarity, a rare model of princely good nature."

This work provides many other problems, and other pleasures. As we have already mentioned, we are before a diptych painted on both the front and the reverse sides. On the front the busts of the Duke and Duchess are portrayed in profile – as on a medal or a coin – facing each other. On the reverse sides, the two sitters are seated upon triumphal carriages and proceed towards each other on a platform which, apart from the stylization of the rocks, appears to be the Sassi di Simone in the Tuscan-Romagna Appennines, belonging to the Montefeltro.

In the portrayal of the Duke and Duchess, Piero had the completely unique audacity to paint the two profiles against a hot, almost palpable, atmospheric landscape which evaporates into the distance. When we consider the difficulty of linking together the foreground of a single portrait with the infinite distance immediately behind it, we realize that certain fundamental characteristics of the art of Piero, when considered individually, appear to belong to very different artistic experiences and phases; whether it is their mathematic harmony, their almost captious physiognomic realism, or their unsurpassed sense of light. The heads of the Duke and Duchess, for example, are constructed on the basis of a fixed, triadic model, according to the scheme diffused by Luca Pacioli. At the same time, the necessity to detach the portraits successfully from the atmospheric, evanescent backdrop led the artist to emphasize warts, wrinkles and frizzy tufts of hair on the face of Federico and to take advantage of the famous incision of his nasal septum and the physiognomic curiosity of his thin lips; almost to the point of hyperrealism. The same necessity led to the excessive use of red in the clothing and hat of the Duke and over-abundance of jewellery in that of the Duchess. No less interesting is the possible implicit symbolism of the diptych. For the moment it is sufficient to remember that the use of the front and the reverse side permitted Piero to exalt the military prowess of the Duke and his joint virtue as administrator. The

portrait of Battista Sforza appears more problematic; the almost alabaster-like luminosity of her complexion supports the theory that the portrait is posthumous.

*The Triumphs and their landscapes*
The most extraordinary aspect of this diptych, however, is the invention of the landscapes on both back and front. Clark wrote that Piero was the greatest living master of perspective; he was a friend of Alberti and must have known his *camera obscura*. But when dealing with the pictorial effect of the light, he realized the superiority of the northern artists and, amongst all his contemporaries, made the most intelligent use of the late fifteenth century vogue for Flemish painting. He assimilated it completely. The splendid lake behind the white horses of the Duke recalls the river landscapes of Van Eyck, but the nature of the landscape and the quality of the light are totally Umbrian and we can still see them today. He painted the light and gentle undulations which continued to inspire Perugino long after his Florentine contemporaries had abandoned any design to paint the surrounding landscape.

The portraits of the Duke and Duchess of Montefeltro – celebrations of the ideals of a highly civilized court – anticipate the last, or almost last, stage of our journey, when it crosses the Apennines beyond San Sepolcro towards Urbino. In this city Piero received many commissions, including the enigmatic *Flagellation* and the *Altar-piece with Federico da Montefeltro*, previously located in the votive church of S. Bernardino and today in the Brera Gallery in Milan. "No learned man would come to Urbino, or to where His Grace was staying, without being honoured by him and invited to be his guest", commented Vespasiano da Bisticci on the hospitable patronage of Federico, who, at the height of his military career and wealth, was patron of the most advanced humanist erudition. Piero always maintained a real sense of gratitude towards this court and in his old age dedicated his treatise *De Quinque Corporibus Regularibus* to the son of Federico, Guidobaldo. From our point of view, however, it

*Beato Angelico, Deposition, Florence, Museum
of S. Marco.*

*Masaccio, The Tribute, Florence, S. Maria del Carmine.*

*Masaccio and Masolino, The Healing of the Cripple and Tabita, Florence, S. Maria del Carmine.*

is opportune to remember that Urbino represented for Piero the possibility of a prolonged contact with one of the most active courts of the day. A court responsible for the patronage of the architecture of Laurana, who set in motion the construction of the "city in the form of a palace", of Flemish painting, which was to have such an influence on Piero through Giusto di Gand, active in Urbino in these years and through a work of Van Eyck, of mathematicians, including his fellow countryman Luca Pacioli, catalyst of European scientific knowledge, not to mention of the prestigious library of Federico.

*The Apprenticeship of Piero*
The profiles of the Duke and Duchess of Urbino and the beautiful landscapes behind present us with an art of complex ancestry; its initial roots are in Florence and its reconstruction can take place through the masterpieces to be found in the city's museums and churches. Berenson notes the influence of Domenico Veneziano in the rendering of the features, of Paolo Uccello in the perspective, of which Piero was himself a fervent student, but above all maintains that Piero was a greater artist than his teachers. He also stresses the importance of Piero's collaboration on the execution of a lost cycle of frescoes by Veneziano in Florence in 1439. It is therefore natural to suggest to the traveller in search of Piero to visit, during the course of his Florentine stay, those works which

influenced his artistic formation and the vivid memory of which was to re-emerge years later in his own works. Our Florentine itinerary will naturally be limited to a few masterpieces of its figurative tradition, with particular attention to the decade 1430 to 1440 – the years of Piero's apprenticeship – although remembering that it was the whole "eclectic" artistic environment which influenced the young artist from Borgo San Sepolcro. The most effective synthesis of Piero's Florentine stay is provided by Battisti: "From the entire works of Piero, it is clear that he studied both the avantguard anti-Gothic and the late Gothic in Florence; he saw Masolino, admired Masaccio, was fascinated by Brunelleschi and showed a lively interest in the fragmentary vision of Paolo Uccello....The manuscript of *Della Pittura* by Leon Battista Alberti, dedicated to Brunelleschi, was circulating amongst artists and Piero, of all the Tuscans, was sure to have read it most carefully....

Moreover, the concept of universality, proportion, rule, the laical atmosphere, the interest in the human figure and its exaltation, and the other elements which characterize Piero at first glance are certainly Florentine".

Our Florentine itinerary begins here: taking as our cue his only work in the Uffizi, our aim is to reconstruct the principle influences on the development of Piero's art.

*Domenico Veneziano*
The Uffizi Gallery offers the unparalleled possibility of studying the *Altar-piece of S. Lucia dei Magnoli*, painted by Domenico Veneziano (circa 1400 – 1461) immediately after the documented evidence of Piero's collaboration. First and foremost, the observer is struck by the use of colour in this work; soft, luminous and sometimes gaudy, it reached Florence through the Venetian painters. There is a new chromatic sensitivity, a completely original perception of atmosphere, a tendency to model the figures and objects by means of reflected light, to establish solid relationships between the coloured figures and the architecture – the portico divided into three

sections substitutes the traditional triptych – which leads to the insertion of this new chromatic and visual experience within a scenic and severely perspective structure.

*Beato Angelico*
In his own way, a painter of the "anti-Gothic avantguard", who had an important influence on Piero. Bewitched by the "innocence" of his colours, we can find it hard to perceive the working presence of new artistic directions in the work of Beato Angelico (circa 1400 – 1455). Two works in the Uffizi serve to demonstrate the singular appearance of a new sensitivity towards light and space even in the mystic and dazzling splendour of his gold grounds. We refer to the *Madonna di Pontassieve*, characterized by the contrast between the sweetness of the flesh tones and the decisive colouring of the clothing, and above all, to the *Incoronation of the Virgin* with its basin-like spatial structure, created by the reduction in size of the figures of the angels and saints, from whose centre rise Christ and the crowned Virgin. As it is easy to imagine, Piero was able to study other works by Angelico even more decisively steeped in the renewed Florentine cultural climate, such as the "modern" *Incoronation of the Virgin* in the Louvre. Nevertheless, our visitor will find a a work of art in the Museum of S. Marco, the *Deposition of Christ*, which already possesses a typical compromise of the young Piero between perspective vision and late Gothic chromatic splendour, between Masaccio and Gentile da Fabriano. The *Deposition* is also fundamental evidence of his unprecedented display of the naive amazement of man who discovers, as though suddenly, the many-formed spectacle of the universe, by whose charm the actual sentiment of the Passion is soothed and made impersonal.

*Masaccio*
Piero's debt to Masaccio (1401 – 1428) – the most innovative artist in the Florentine circle – is summarized in the clearest and most effective terms by Clark: "...it was the prolonged contemplation of the Carmine frescoes themselves which moulded his style. From them he learnt the majestic

*Masaccio, S. Anna, the Madonna and Child,*
*Florence, Uffizi.*

34

*Masaccio, The Holy Trinity, Florence, S. Maria Novella.*

*Gentile da Fabriano, S. Maria Maddalena,*
*S. Nicola da Bari, Quaratesi, Polyptych,*
*Florence, Uffizi.*

*Gentile da Fabriano, S. Giovanni Battista,*
*S. Giorgio, Quaratesi, Polyptych, Florence,*
*Uffizi.*

38

tempo, the grave gestures, the vision of an ennobled humanity, which characterize all his work. And on the technical side he learnt the architecture of drapery and the grouping of figures in space". We are better able to understand Masaccio by studying his panel depicting *St. Anne, the Madonna, the Child and five angels* in which the distinction – already suggested by Longhi – between the painting of the central group by Masaccio and that of the surrounding figures by Masolino da Panicale appears quite clear. The central group consists of one single block, cemented together in a plastic and psychological cohesion which finds its confirmation in the physical presence of the figures and their firm scansion in human time.

We cannot fail at this point to suggest a visit to two works by Masaccio which represent the peak of Florentine early renaissance painting: the *Trinity* in Santa Maria Novella, in which a brunelleschian vault holds the mystery of the Trinity within its tangible space, and the cycle of frescoes in the Brancacci chapel in Santa Maria del Carmine, where Masaccio together with Masolino (1383 circa – 1440) painted the *Miracles of St. Peter*. In these scenes, famous for their essentiality and vigour, "the

bodies solidly occupy their own defined space, throwing real shadows on the ground" – as it has been observed – whereas their surroundings, whether incumbent hilly landscapes or severe townscapes, correspond to the narrated events. When studying the frescoes of the *Legend of the Cross* by Piero della Francesca, we cannot help remembering the "majestic tense" of Masaccio, his ability to provide enormous significance to the groups of figures in daily scenes.

*Paolo Uccello*

Amongst the great innovators of the Florentine era, Piero did not fail to admire Paolo Uccello (1397 – 1475) – in particular the frescoes in the Chapel of the Assunta in the Duomo of Prato – following his own interest in mathematics. The ostentatious perspective vision of Paolo Uccello is like a mathematic truth in which the framing of the empiric world acquires the unreal atmosphere of a fable. The *Battle of St. Romano* in the Uffizi – almost contemporary with Piero's frescoes in Arezzo - demonstrates how his rigorous study of perspective of figures, animals and objects placed within space creates a visual fragmentation which increases the sense of the

*Agnolo Gaddi, Legend of the Cross: the Jews find the wood from which they make the Cross, Florence, S. Croce.*

*Agnolo Gaddi, Discovery and Proof of the true Cross, Florence, S. Croce.*

40

unreal. Isolated in space, in fact, the forms reveal essential geometric structures quite different from those which we perceive in their actual daily existence. The colours become qualities of the perspective planes and not of the objects; the fields, therefore, can be "blue" and the cities "red in colour", as Vasari remarks with irony. Without the "sweet folly" of Paolo Uccello's perspective, however, we would probably not have Piero's rigorous detachment when dealing with figures, events and objects in a world which is heraldically and geometrically essential, made out of spheres, cubes and cylinders, yet brought to life by the light of its composed monumentality.

However wide and fascinating the range of references in the Uffizi available to the visitor who wishes to provide himself with both expertise and enjoyment in this pilgrimage to Piero della Francesca, a list of too many references cannot fail to be disturbing. We will, therefore, only point out a few other comparative works, which will make our approach to the Arezzo cycle and to the artist's work in his place of birth, and residence, easier and more productive.

*Gentile da Fabriano*
Amongst the paintings of the Uffizi, it is worthwhile considering two masterpieces in the rear-guard of Florentine art of the first half of the fifteenth century; the *Adoration of the Magi* and the *Quaratesi polytypch* by Gentile da Fabriano (circa 1370 – circa 1427). Piero was influenced by the gentle luminosity, the delicacy of the modelling, the detailed representation of the dazzling, quilted robes and the landscapes of this artist's work, in the so-called "international Gothic" style. On the other hand, there is a singular and totally personal continuity between Piero's preference for the conventional descriptive nature of the Gothic and his increasingly intense love of Flemish painting; both are inspired by an effective anxiety to describe and to define. The words of Clark explain well this paradoxical fascination of Piero, an artist of impassive synthesis, for Flemish art: "Piero's interest in Flemish painting, which lasted throughout his life, and increased during his later years, seems, at first, to be incompatible with the classic and geometric basis of his art: but in fact it springs from the same conception of art as a form of knowledge. His temperament inclined him to the abstract knowledge of mathematics, but he was sufficiently a painter to value the empirical knowledge of perception, and he recognized that, in this branch, Flemish painters had surpassed those in Italy".

*Roger van der Weyden and Hugo van der Goes*
Still within the Uffizi, we cannot fail to note the extraordinary *Deposition and Entombment* by Roger van der Weyden (circa 1400 – 1464) – an artist who met Piero in Ferrara in 1449 – with its detailed descriptive landscape and the tactile presence of the materials, figures and hair, and the *Portinari triptych with the Adoration of the Shepherds* by Hugo van der Goes (1440 – 1482), an artist known to Piero before this work through Giusto di Gand in Urbino.

*Donatello and Ghiberti*
It will be clear to the reader by now the

*Hugo van der Goes, Central part of the
Portinari Triptych, Florence, Uffizi.*

extent of the complicated web of relationships, exchanges and influences interwo-
ven into the art of Piero, who is considered
nevertheless one of the most original and
individual artists in the history of art. Yet
we must remember that the works mentioned in the Uffizi should be viewed in
relation to the *entire* range of Piero's
works. Our traveller should, therefore,
stay a little longer in Florence to view
other works from that figurative tradition
so important to Piero. He should also make
a note to re-visit the stages in this artist's
formation at the end of his trip, if possible,
in order to "fix" the essential examples in
his memory. To reduce the comparisons to
a minimum, we will only consider a few
essential cases. We have already mentioned the revolutionary presence of Ma-

saccio and the affrescoes in the Carmine.
In following a straightforward tourist's
route through the city, the visitor will
come across other examples of fifteenth
century Florentine art to have directly
influenced the work of Piero and we will
refer to these in Arezzo and San Sepolcro:
the *Gates of Paradise* of the Baptistry of S.
Maria del Fiore with the *plaques* by Lorenzo Ghiberti, the *equestrian frescoes* by Paolo Uccello and Andrea di Castagna in the
same cathedral, Alberti's *facade* for Santa
Maria Novella and the *St. George* by Donatello in the Bargello, whose posture was to
be echoed in Piero's prophets for the Arezzo cycle.

*Andrea del Castagno*
Two evocative visits remain in this itiner-

*Piero della Francesca, Nativity, detail of the*
*Child.*
*(to be compared with)*
*Hugo van der Goes, Portinari Triptych, detail*
*of the Child.*

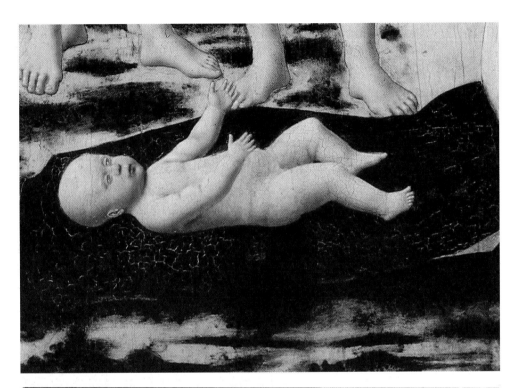

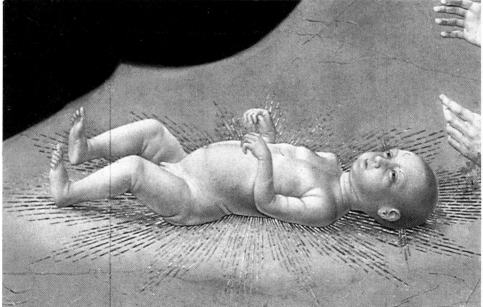

*Beato Angelico, Deposition, detail with a view
of the city.
(to be compared with)*

*Piero della Francesca, View of the city of
Arezzo, from the Proof of the True Cross.*

*Gentile da Fabriano, Adoration of the Magi,*
*Florence, Uffizi.*

44

*Agnolo Gaddi, Decapitation of Chosroes and the return of Herclius to Jerusalem with the True Cross, Florence, S. Croce.*

ary, both for those who wish to deepen their knowledge of the cultural, or simply iconic, climate in which Piero worked, and those who wish to appreciate them for their own qualities as exemplary moments in a great artistic tradition. We refer to the *Cenacolo di S. Apollonia* with the frescoes of Andrea del Castagna (circa 1419 – 1457), representing the *Last Supper* and the *Resurrection*, in which the very synthesis of humanist and christian values, repeated once more in Piero, seem to take bodily form. The geometric structure confers absolute quality of form on this synthesis, subordinated to the disturbing linear excavations.

## Agnolo Gaddi

The other visit is to the church of S. Croce, in which it is helpful to see the fresco cycle in the main chapel dedicated to the *Legend of the Cross* (1374 – 1395) by Agnolo Gaddi

(circa 1350 – 1396), a theme which recurs frequently in the mural cycles of Franciscan churches in Tuscany before Piero. It is clear that Gaddi belonged neither to the cultural climate which affected Piero's formation, nor to the group of artists who influenced the development of his genius. However, it is worthwhile comparing his pictorial cycle with that of Piero in the theme and scansion of the narrative sequence and its significant variations.

## Leaving Florence

Before leaving Florence for Arezzo through the gate of S. Niccolò, as was once the custom, we should pause in one of the most famous Florentine cafes. On arrival, we followed the logistic indications of an Englishman almost contemporary with Shakespeare, but at the moment before our departure, let us be guided by a young American, De Forest, who stayed in Flo-

*Beato Angelico, Madonna with Child, Florence, Uffizi.*

rence during the reign of the last Granduke: "Cafe Doney was just the same thing as ever, from the three saloons, the cream-colored columns, and the marble-topped tables, to the white uniforms of the Austrian officers, the easy traveling coats of the English tourists, and the noisy waiters, rushing about like incarnations of perpetual motion, and shouting the orders of the guests with the vehemence of sea-captains in a hurricane. Giovanni, the good-natured fellow whose particular duty it was to pour out the coffee, came up to us with a grin of friendly recognition on his face, a huge coffee-pot of welcome in his hand, and a hospitable vessel of hot milk in the other.

"Good-morning to these gentlemen," said Giovanni. "They are welcome to Florence. I hope they have had a pleasant journey. What will they take for breakfast?"

Once it was necessary to travel on the mail coach to Rome in order to reach Arezzo, or to hire a carriage with coachman. Stendhal gives the following advice in his *Useful Guide for Those Travelling in Italy*: "Look for Marchioni who lives in Florence near the Boboli gardens; a boy will accompany you there for two *crazie*; say to Signor Marchioni: 'Signore, I wish to go to Rome via Perugia' ....One can also take the diligence for Perugia which stops a hundred yards from the customs, on the east side of the equestrian statue (of Ferdinand I, in piazza SS. Annunziata), the fee is very reasonable .... One can also go via Siena, but the journey through Perugia and Arezzo is by far the most interesting."

*J. Pennell, Via Porta Rossa, illustration for Henry James, Italian Hours, 1909.*

*J. Pennell, Houses on the Arno, 1909.*

*J. Pennell, Piazza S. Maria Novella, 1909.*

*J. Pennell, View of Florence from Boboli, 1909.*

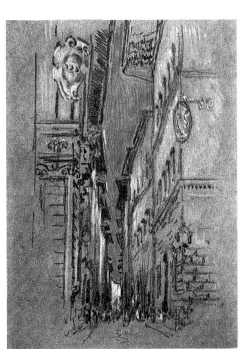

48

*"The Appennines, which rose in
the distance, were covered with
snow, yet the trees had scarcely
lost their foliage, as if the
parting Autumn 'its lingering
bloom delay'd', and the mid-day
sun fell in rays of gold on the
dark and distant fir-forests of
Vallombrosa"*

Lady Morgan.

*A part of the Grand Tour*

Arezzo can be reached directly by train, or
by the motorway A1. However, the experi-
enced traveller or lover of the picturesque
can follow – or keep in mind for another
occasion – the old Aretine road (SS 67 to
Pontassieve, then SS 69 Valdarno) which
winds along the Arno in a stretch of ex-
traordinarily unchanged and beautiful
landscape. An editor of the most popular
tourist guides of the first half of the nine-
teeth century, William Brockedon, makes
the following measured, and still relevant,
comments: "The drive by Pontassieve is
very beautiful: the mountains which
bound the valley approach nearer: the
wooded hills round Vallombrosa, and the
mountain-ridge which separates the traveller from Camaldoli, are rich and beautiful features in the landscapes of the valley,
which is highly cultivated, and abounds in
neat villas and villages."

It is in this first part of the route that one
finds the road to the Monastery of Vallombrosa. In differing centuries, both John
Milton, who drew inspiration for the *Para-*

*dise Lost*, and the restless Mary Shelley
wandered in these forests and Louis Gauf-
fier and Philipp Hackert passed hours
painting in its glades. We cross the Arno at
Incisa. Brockedon writes, " The road
thence continues along the left bank of the
Arno through Figline, San Giovanni, and
Montevarchi, amidst scenes of great rich-
ness, and a luxuriance of vegetation
scarcely surpassed elsewhere in Italy. The
mountain-slopes produce some of the finest wines; and the proprietors appear to be
opulent and independent....The road then
traverses Lavane, and gradually leaves the
Arno on the left. A basin in the Appennines, formed between the great chain and
the Monte Prato-Magno, in which lies the
source of the Arno, encloses in its deep and
secluded recesses the famous monasteries
of Camaldoli and La Verna; places of pilgrimage to the lovers of wild and picturesque scenery, but too far removed and
difficult of access for common-place sight-
hunters." Both have their place in the
artistic development of Piero and his future destiny. As we will see, Camaldoli, in
particular, held an extremely important
political and cultural position in his day.

Even the most hurried traveller using either the motorway or the train can still
enjoy views like those lovingly described
by Lady Morgan in 1819 in her guide: "The
scenery from Florence to Incisa is that of
an English garden; and some of the many
villas, viewed at a little distance, resemble
the old mansions-seats of Queen Anne's
time".

*The Journey from Florence to Arezzo,*
*following the pilgrims' routes, from Guida per*
*viaggiar la Toscana, XVIIIth century.*

*The main roads between Florence and the Val*
*di Chiana, from Guida per viaggiar la*
*Toscana, XVIIIth century.*

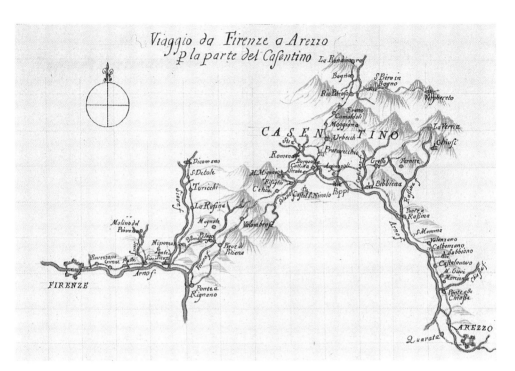

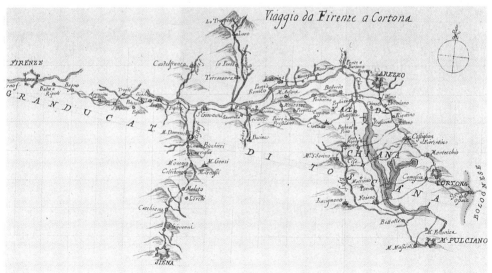

*Timetable for the mail coach.*

*Ticket for the mail coach.*

50    *Historic inns*

We have now arrived in that final stretch of Tuscany, which inspired Stendhal to advise his readers to make a stock of wine and cheese before crossing the papal border, and which Goethe praised for its olives and the cultiviation of the Chiana. It seems an opportune moment, therefore, to reconstruct the lodgings and the meals provided in the inns of the past. There is plenty of documentary evidence on this subject, since the route between Florence and Arezzo formed part of the itinerary of the Grand Tour; this "trip" was undertaken by wealthy aristocrats and entrepreneurial bourgeois from all of Europe, from the sixteenth to the nineteenth centuries. It was considered a form of "finishing school" after studies and personal education, a chance to collect and to study the market, and a fashionable entertainment. This road is anyway a part of the route between Florence and Rome, a route which goes through Arezzo to Perugia and South Umbria, an alternative to the more troubled route along the via Francigena through Siena.

To take this route once again, on roads little changed from their original form, signifies following in the footsteps of intellectuals, diplomats, writers – men and women – who have analytically described its nature. Travel literature, from that of the pilgrims of Chaucer directed to Canterbury to the nocturnal wayfarers of Calvino, has taught us that there is as much interest to be found in the lodgings, as in the journey itself, so it would not be out of place to refer to some descriptive passages of inns situated along the route in question. The great English novelist, Tobias Smollett, with his habitual black humour, and this time perhaps with reason, wrote in 1764: "The house (Pian della Fonte?) was dismal and dirty beyond all description; the bed-clothes filthy enough to turn the stomach of a muleteer; and the victuals cooked in such a manner, that even a Hottentot could not have beheld them without loathing. We had sheets of our own, which were spread upon a mattrass, and here I took my repose wrapped in a greatcoat, if that could be called repose

# DILIGENZA
## GIORNALIERA
## DA FIRENZE AD AREZZO
### E VICEVERSA

A principiare dal dì                    184

| PARTENZA DA FIRENZE | | PARTENZA DA AREZZO | |
|---|---|---|---|
| Lunedì | | Lunedì | |
| Martedì | | Martedì | |
| Mercoledì | di ogni Settimana | Mercoledì | di ogni Settimana |
| Giovedì | | Giovedì | |
| Venerdì | | Venerdì | |
| Sabato ma a ore | | Sabato ma a ore | |

### PREZZO DEI POSTI

| Coupé | . . | Lire 8. | . . | Coupé | . . . | Lire 8. | . . |
|---|---|---|---|---|---|---|---|
| Interno | . . . | „ 6. 13. 4. | | Interno | . . . | „ 6. 13. 4. |
| Rotonda | . . . | „ 5. „ „ | | Rotonda | . . . | „ 5. „ „ |
| Panchetta | . . . | „ 5. „ „ | | Panchetta | . . . | „ 5. „ „ |

### STRADALE

| Incisa | . . . | £ 2. 13. 4. | | Levane | . . . | £ 2. 13. 4. |
|---|---|---|---|---|---|---|
| Figline | . . . | „ 2. 13. 4. | | Montevarchi | . . . | „ 2. 13. 4. |
| S. Giovanni | . | „ 3. 6. 8. | | S. Giovanni | . | „ 3. 6. 8. |
| Montevarchi | . | „ 4. - - | | Figline | . . . | „ 4. - - |

Arezzo 1847 Tip. Bellotti

# DILIGENZA
## DA FIRENZE AD AREZZO, E VICEVERSA

| PIAZZA FISSATA | NUM. DELLA PIAZZA | PARTENZA | | DESTINO | PREZZO PAGATO |
|---|---|---|---|---|---|
| | | GIORNO | ORE | | |
| Berlina | 3. | il 29. Giugno il dì 1847 | 7. di Mattina | Firenze | £ 6. 13. 4 |

N. B. Mancando il Viaggiatore all'ora stabilita per la Partenza, perde il prezzo del Posto.

*John Warwick Smith, View of the Upper Valley of the Arno, engraving, 1780.*   *John D. Harding, View of Pelago, from The Tourist in Italy, 1832.*

51

*J. D. Harding, View of Vallombrosa,*
*from The Tourist in Italy, 1832.*

*E. Bury, View of Vallombrosa, from The Three*
*Great Sanctuaries of Tuscany, 1833.*

*E. Bury, View of Camaldoli, 1833.*

*E. Bury, View of Verna, 1833.*

which was interrupted by the innumerable stings of vermin. In the morning, I was seized with a dangerous fit of hooping-cough... This forenoon, one of our coach wheels flew off in the neighbourhood of Ancisa". Conditions were no better in Incisa a century later, even though a sojourn in this town could be amusing and fascinating, as the French artist De Mercey noted in 1858: "We stopped for dinner in Incisa, a lively town and gateway to the upper Valdarno. Having dined miserably in a hovel like those in the suburbs of Florence, we paid the inn-keeper and proceeded to paint the view of the city dominated by a fortress, in its turn surmounted by a high tower."

At the beginning of the nineteenth century, the romantic poet, Samuel Rogers, does not seem to hold in high regard the inn at Levane, and cites Horace from his Brindisi voyage: "We slept at Levane: 'lacrimoso non sine fumo'". Lady Morgan provides us with a lively sketch of the same inn: "At the *Locanda of Levane*, we found all with-

*Romayne Robert, View of Incisa,
travel note-book, circa 1896.*

INCISA

in and without its walls the very picturesque of dreariness; and the boisterous manners of our young and handsome female attendants curiously contrasted with their dilatory movements; for though all our requests were answered with *'Subito, subito'* – nothing could be less *'subito'* than their services, notwithstanding the remonstrances of our Florentine servant, who seemed to know how to deal with them". It should be mentioned that centuries beforehand, an inn in the same neighbourhood had enchanted the great traveller Montaigne, who was certainly not easy to please. "Levanella: the locanda is to be found about one mile before the village and is famous; it is considered the best in Tuscany and rightly so. Here they prepare great bonfires, and they say that the local nobility often use it as a meeting place, like the 'Moro' in Paris, or the 'Guillot' in Amiens. They use tin plates, which is quite unique. The house stands by itself, in a superb position as regards the plane, with a spring of water for its own use".

*The road to Ancona*
Let us not forget that at the time of Montaigne, the route between Florence and Arezzo, and therefore between Arezzo and San Sepolcro, already formed part of the so-called "road to Ancona". We are reminded of this by the German geographer, Joseph Furttenbach in 1607: "Every Sunday, a coach leaves from Florence for Ancona on payment of six *piastre*. This does not only transport its passengers using robust mules, who are without doubt more secure than horses for climbing the mountains, but it also sustains the traveller for the five day journey to Ancona....In Florence there is also the possibility of hiring horses. These are hired out for weeks on end, together with a guide, expert in the roads and paths, who precedes the traveller on horseback …".

*Aretine valleys*
To discover the Aretine area also signifies visually discovering one of the communi-

55

cation knots of central Italy through which much knowledge has passed. Until the late Middle Ages, the Casentino, a valley which appears the most secluded and wooded today, was crossed by pilgrims on their way to Rome, as an alternative to the route following the valley of the Tiber. Subsequent to the reclamation of the swampy Val di Chiana by the Grandukes of Tuscany, the Arezzo road was used increasingly often by travellers on the Grand Tour to reach the heart of Umbria, and then to Rome. We have already discussed the Adriatic route.

To think of Arezzo, therefore, is to think of its valleys, which modern tourists have discovered with such delight: the routes along the Valdarno with its towns and parishes on the back of the Pratomagno, the Val di Chiana with its Etruscan and Mediaeval fortresses, Castiglio Fiorentino, Montecchio, Cortona, Lucignano, which still seem to lean forward, like arks of history, over the glassy marsh, or the Case-

ntino with its easy access to the famous monasteries of Camaldoli and della Verna, which tourists once reached from Vallombrosa, and finally the Valtiberina of Piero della Francesca.

In this prilgimage to Piero we can but limit ourselves to a mention of places, which a more detailed research would immediately bring into the foreground. To take just one example, the Chief Abbot of the monastery of Camaldoli was Ambrogio Traversari, the famous humanist, who campaigned until his death in 1439 for the reconciliation of the Western with the Greek church; since Traversari was also Superintendent of the Camaldolese Badia of San Sepolcro, later the cathedral, he could well have influenced Piero's iconographic choices. Every inch of these valleys and mountains has been a fleeting or unconscious witness to the history of Piero or his work. But ours is but a guide, travelling on four wheels, at the mercy of the postilion and the untiring postman.

56

*"I stayed in Arezzo and became
an accepted local figure. My
work was done in the morning,
when the Church was empty;
and by 4.30, when smart people
began arriving from Florence, I
was seated at the café
overlooking piazza S. Francesco,
and could witness the short
visits payed by social figures."*

Sir Kenneth Clark, 1946

*Views of the city*
We refer to one of the most recent travel
writers, André Suarès, for a complete picture of Arezzo as it first appears to the
modern tourist: "Full of life, facing the soft
hills, Arezzo seems like a hand rising and
spreading over the heights: the great
thumb pointing to the Levant, as far as the
stadium, where man enjoys himself by
playing ball with his feet, the little finger
stretched out towards Florence, on the
side of the porta S. Lorentino. At the foot
of the hills, the slender wrist supports the
palm of the narrow streets, which climb
towards the cathedral and the gardens.
Neither young, nor old, Arezzo has an
antique atmosphere, an indefinable mock-
ing quality, not exactly mediaeval or even
decadent. The whole city has the intelligent appearance of the late Renaissance."
Only cities which impress the imagination
with their physiognomy can count on a
metaphor of such eloquence. The initial
appearance of historic Arezzo, in fact, co-
incides with Piero's typically topographical view of the city painted on the walls of
S. Francesco.

*Echoes of famous travellers*
It is usual to approach Arezzo from the
open space before the cathedral, as William Weaver advised some years ago: "A
good rule with Italian hill towns is to begin
at the top, especially if you are on foot
(and sightseeing, after all, is really a pedestrian activity). You get your climbing over
with at the start, and afterwards it is
downhill all the way. With Arezzo, a southern Tuscan city I visit often, the rule works

fairly well." Before entering the cathedral
for our first meeting with Piero della Francesca, we should walk into the wide,
neighbouring, "Liberty" style garden – "il
Prato" – between the cathedral apse and
the Medici fortress. This offers a marvel-
lous view over the valley and the foothills
of the Apennines to the North-East, and
over the city to the South-West: a viewpoint enjoyed by entire groups of tourists.
"In Arezzo, you are always aware of the
city's natural context, its place in the
wider landscape ", Weaver continues, un-
consciously echoing a splendid topographical reflection of Walter Pater in 1872:
"You know those days when although the
sun is hidden yet it is not far behind the
clouds and brings out in the cooler light a
thousand colours else unperceived.
(Around us lies) the very image of a land of
hope, the watery sunlight falling on its
distant level spaces, its hollows indicated
only by shades of deeper blue. The Ape-
nines which encircle you on three sides are
not too importunate as you catch them up
some narrow street or deserted courtway.
Their outlines, outlines of singular beauty
and vigour seem drawn in half angry cloud
only along the horizon. The plain below
opens with something of width and space
leaving room for the play of many lights
among its scattered vineyards, and in the
clear air every detail even in extreme distance – the strange small fields of ripened
maize, the threshing-floor below where
you can see, and might count, each stock
of yellow straw – lies distinctly visible,
only diminished by distance bringing an
impression of infinite clearness and delicacy, like the work of some fine etches.
On this side the hill of Arezzo sinks abrupt-
ly to the plain with crumbling walls and
aged chestnut trees whose great motion-
less leaves seem wrought in bronze. On the
other side lies Arezzo itself, sloping so
steeply that the open stages of the tall
Lombard tower of Santa Maria del Pieve,
in the Piazza below look close at hand, and
the broad streets with their yellow house-
fronts and smooth bleached pavements
seem to dip quite suddenly right away into
the distant blue."
Many years later, at the beginning of this

W. Brockedon, *View of Arezzo, From London
to Naples. A Road-book, 1832.*

J. Gourdault, *View of Arezzo, from Les villes
de la Toscane, 1888.*

century, another visitor, Olave M. Potter, travelling together with a very fine Japanese engraver, Yoshio Markino, noticed the particular characteristics of the place and also the lines of urban development beyond the city walls, towards the plain: "She has left her hill-top now that she needs no more the walls which Sangallo built in the fighting days of the Popes, and has trailed down to the railway in the valley,leaving behind her wide piazzas which she has filled with shady trees, and benches, and statues of her great ones. Her paved streets, steep and clean, climb up the hill-side between grey palaces, green-shuttered, with wide Tuscan eaves, whose fantastic outlines, seen in échelon against the sky, bring back a score of memories of other clean-swept Tuscan towns." Arezzo is no longer the torpid city which troubled Lady Morgan with its superstition and squalor: "We found its narrow and dirty streets crowded with beggars, chequered by petty venders of fruit and maccaroni; and there was little to induce the most inquiring traveller to pause beyond the

58

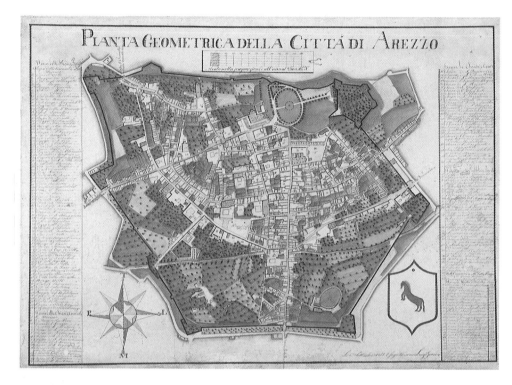

time necessarily given to its few and neglected historical buildings". Neither is it the mysterious and fascinating city of Henry James, who made it the prototype of Italian hill cities, the true relics of history: "leaving the dust of the ages unfingered on the stored records ...in that case indeed the story assaults him but from too many sides ...at moments I feel that I must sneak along on tiptoe in order not to have to much of it." The tourist's modern Arezzo has even less in common with the city, which Tobias Smollett passed through in 1764: "The fifth night we passed at a place called Camoccia, a miserable cabaret, where we were fain to cook our own supper, and lay in a musty chamber, which had never known a fire, and indeed had no fire-place, and where we ran the risk of being devoured by rats. Next day one of the irons of the coach gave way at Arezzo, where we were detained two hours before it could be accomodated. I might have taken this opportunity to view the remains

of the ancient Etruscan amphitheatre, and the temple of Hercules, described by the cavalier Lorenzo Guazzesi, as standing in the neighbourhood of this place: but the blacksmith assured me his work would be finished in a few minutes; and as I had nothing so much at heart as the speedy accomplishment of this disagreeable journey, I chose to suppress my curiosity, rather than be the occasion of a moment's delay."

Again Weaver observes that today Arezzo is rather more than the sum total of its historic monuments: "I like it because it is not a tourist city. Visitors are welcome, but they are not fawned upon. The Aretini get on with their job. This is really an industrial city: Arezzo's ready-made men's clothes are exported widely, and the manufacture of inexpensive jewelery (holy medals, wedding rings) is a local specialty." This does not mean, however, as the American magazine "Travel and Leisure" points out, that this city does not hold a particular

*Topographical plan of Arezzo, circa 1830.*

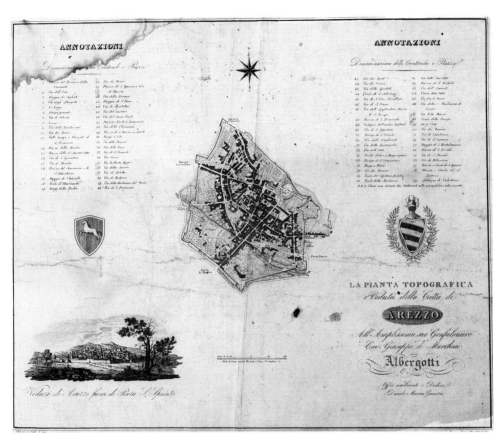

enchantment, which is changing and active, yet stationary, at the same time: "Arezzo is more than a mere town, on somewhat less than a hill. Hill town or not, it backs right up into the Apennines, as is readily apparent from the lovely Prato (park) behind the Duomo. With about 100.000 inhabitants, Arezzo is one of those endearing little Italian cities where, despite some earnest urban pretensions, rural life still intrudes. Not 300 yards from the Palazzo Comunale (city hall) the vineyards begin, and it is not unusual to hear a cackling rooster remind the town of its early agricultural origins".

*The first meeting with Piero: the Magdalene*
Our first meeting with Piero della Francesca in Arezzo takes place within the cathedral before the fresco of the *Magdalene*. The cathedral was often described during the course of the eighteenth and nineteenth centuries both as a whole – "We found the Cathedral very stately with its great arches, and darkly magnificent with the dim rich light coming through its painted windows", as Hawthorne observes, – and for its single works of art, such as the beautiful windows of Guglielmo di Marcillat, or the funeral monument of the bellicose Bishop Tarlati. "The tomb of Guido (Tarlati) is a monument to power, a reminder of the violence and strife of the Middle Ages here", writes Weaver, who then continues: "but next to it is a reminder of Renaissance grace and beauty: a little fresco of the Magdalene by Piero della Francesca. There is a sense of mystery about this lone, isolated figure, whose cool

*Plan of Arezzo, 1900.*

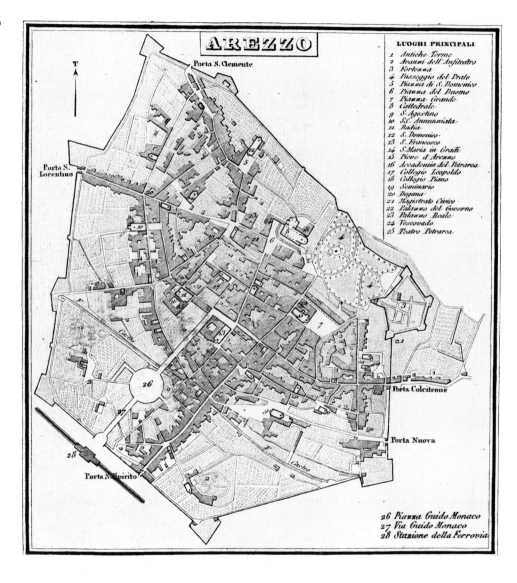

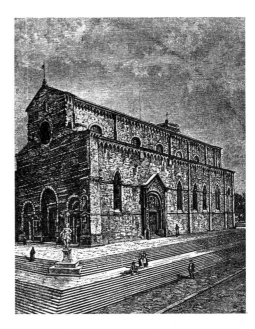

61

elegance glows as if eternally caught by a patch of sunlight." From 1842, the year in which the first annotation of a foreign traveller is to be found, up to today, it is difficult to find a fresher and in its own way, more truthful impression of this painting. For the art historians, from Longhi onwards, the *Magdalene*, fruit of Piero's full maturity, is one of his greatest works of art. The marked originality of the fresco should not be separated from a perceptible echo of the most significant moments of renaissance art. Maria Magdalene is figured in audacious perspective against a blue sky, framed within an architrave decorated with patterns from classical Greece. The whites of the architectural frame and the lining of the mantle contrast strongly with the green and the red, as though illuminated by a "patch of sunlight". The artist's use of white and grey reaches such effective heights of virtuosity in the crystal vase, which stands out against the figure with its shadows and its transparence, that it suggests Flemish influence. In the physiognomy of the face, like many other female figures by Piero della Francesca, the *Magdalene* might seem "more magisterial than poetic", as Clark notes, even if a subtle difference between the two eyes seems to hint at an imperceptible, humane melancholy.

*S. Francesco in the nineteenth century*
Between the nineteenth and twentieth centuries, foreign visitors to Arezzo usually stayed at the Grand Hotel d'Angleterre next to the church of S. Francesco in the square of that name. "We are staying in the Hotel d'Angleterre, to make a change", writes Theodor Mommsen in 1845, "the food is better than elsewhere and the Montepulciano we ordered was very good". But strange as it seems, almost nobody entered the church to view the *Legend of the Cross*. Piero, as we have already mentioned, is a discovery of our century. On the other hand, the almost continual closure of the church of S. Francesco, whether for reasons of safety, or for transformation and restoration, did not encourage the occasional curiosity of travellers, who were led by contemporary taste to admire

62

the *Marriage of Esther and Assuero* of
Vasari, and ignore artists prior to Raphael.
The few foreign visitors who managed to
penetrate the interior of the church, which
was, incidentally, twice assigned as military quarters during the course of the
eighteenth century, describe the frescoes
of Piero in an extreme state of disrepair, as
Lord Lindsay wrote in 1842.

*The first visitors*
Let us follow in the footsteps of a few of
these rare visitors to the inaccessible
church of S. Francesco and listen to their
expressions of disappointment and sur-
prise before the frescoes of Piero. Around
1845, the historian of the Dukes of Montefeltro, Sir James Denistoun, makes a series
of pertinent comments concerning the art
of Piero and the condition of the paintings:
"These noble works, uniting a happy appli-
cation of his favourite studies on perspective and light, with a grandeur and movement unknown to most of his compositions, are now mere wrecks, in which,
however, may be traced not a few ideas
subsequently appropriated by more celebrated artists.... The elements have con-
spired against this *chef-d'oeuvre* of Pietro
del Borgo. Its walls were frightfully riven
during last century by an earthquake, and
its menacing cracks have since been shak-
en by thunderbolts. Although the repairs
have been judiciously limited to securing
the plaster, without attempting any restoration of the frescoes, several compart-
ments are almost wholly defaced. Some
female groups, however, remain, which
yield to nothing that Masaccio has left for
the plaudits of posterity." The American
lawyer and excellent writer, Egerton R.
Williams, on a visit in 1903, left a less
professional and more emotional testimony, even though it does not lack fairly
lively tourist comments: "In the Piazza
Umberto is the principal inn, and beside it
the old gothic church of San Francesco,
where morning service was going on at a
side-altar as I entered. The interior consists
of a lofty nave, without aisles or transepts,
having one chapel, opening on the left, and
a slightly elevated choir .....Threading the
crowd of kneeling worshipers amid the

*Piero della Francesca, The Magdalene, Arezzo,*
*Cathdral.*

64

monotonous chant of the priest, I made my way to the chapel on the left, which Spinello once decorated with frescoes, but found them too much injured to be intelligible. Better things were in the choir, adorned on both walls with a great series of scenes from the legend of the Holy Cross by Piero della Francesca , the early quattrocentist master of Luca Signorelli. He is the principal artist to be studied here, as at his neighbouring native town of Sansepulcro. These frescoes .....portray a great many figures in dramatic action, which, for the period (1450), is remarkably well sustained. But the movement shows the same frenzy of energy and lack of grace that we find in most of Signorelli's works. In these few powerful undraped figures by Piero, we also see where Signorelli got his power of executing the nude". The following year, the English writer Maurice Hewlett, author of an excellent publication on Tuscan roads, illustrated by the artist and engraver, Joseph Pennell, added some vivid observations on his visit to Arezzo: "A great painter came to Arezzo from Borgo

over the hill, filled the choir of San Francesco with pageantry, and got much quiet, painter's happiness in between. This was Piero della Francesca. The *Invention of the True Cross*, for that is his theme, gives occasion for all that is expected of a fresco painter of tastes heraldic and processional – a varied story, solemn disputations of great folk, war-pieces with banners and flying horsemen, buildings, distant prospects, and as much familiar detail as you choose. It is a great and a good story, which begins with Adam in Eden, and ends with Heraclius at the Battle of the Danube. It has tempted all sorts of men, for its has murder enough for Matteo of Siena....there are fine ladies for Ghirlandaio; angels, wise merchants, and saucy boys for Benozzo Gozzoli; and for Paolo Uccello big-bellied Flemish horses and spears against the sky.....One may take it that the trappings only interested him as a set-off to his landscape. That is exquisitely beautiful and true. His palette is the nearest to Tuscany of any painter before him or since. Looked at from that standpoint, these frescoes are masterpieces." In 1908, the American collector, Dan Fellows Platt fleetingly mentioned: "At the time of our visit, the church was undergoing a thorough restoration and the frescoes were in anything but a fit setting. Nevertheless, the direct sincerity of these sturdy representations of Solomon, Constantine and Chosroes did not fail to attract us stongly.". More significantly, the young art historian, P. G. Konody, described a visit which took place in 1911 at the end of the restoration of the entire church complex. He provides an account of the work in course and observations on the art of Piero della Francesca, which seem quite "modern" for the era in which they were written: "All our troubles and discomforts were forgotten when a few minutes later we stood in the choir of San Francesco among the frescoes of our beloved Piero dei Franceschi. The delight was the greater, as it was altogether unexpected, for the church, completely dismantled for restoration, and filled with scaffoldings and heaps of debris, presented so dreary an aspect from the entrance that we were

65

half inclined to turn away without passing through the nave, had not an interesting early fresco on the entrance wall induced us to search for more. And so we came to the choir which Piero decorated with the Legend of the Holy Cross – the "Golden Legend", which can here be read from the planting of the branch from the Tree of Knowledge over Adam's grave to the Victory of Constantine over Maxentius – a fragmentary pictorial tale, owing to the havoc wrought by time and damp, but set forth with such power and monumental directness by this master of form and composition, movement and light, that it would be difficult to find its equal in the whole history of art. One has to visit Arezzo if one would realize the full significance and influence of Piero dei Franceschi upon all future art, an influence as great as that exercised by Masaccio. What Masaccio did for form and statuesque grandeur of design, Piero achieved for light and atmosphere. He may be called the discoverer of sunlight and the forerunner of the nineteenth century plein-air school. Nor is there ever in the whole range of his work a concession to prettiness. His types – even the heads of the Queen of Sheba and her women in one of the frescoes at Arezzo – are anything but "pretty": they have the beauty of character and strength and of intense vitality."

### Arezzo in Piero's day

The city of Arezzo, to which Piero was called to paint the main chapel of S. Francesco, from the 1430's onwards was an integral part of the dominion of the Medici, who rose to definitive power in Florence in 1430. Over the years, the power of the Medici was consolidated in the various conquered territories – Arezzo, Pisa, Pistoia and Siena – notwithstanding some attempts at revolt and ephemeral republican resipiscence. The celebrated Battle of Anghiari (1440) ensured the Medici the upper valley of the Tiber and the area of San Sepolcro. The economic life of Arezzo, like other Tuscan territories, registers a flexion in relation to the levels reached the century before. A flexion reflected in the decrease in population. A solid group of families, however, continued a flourishing

66 trade at an inter-regional level. From the beginning of the century, some Aretine merchants, such as the Bacci and the Ubertini, placed themselves, with authoritative wisdom, within the commercial and economic network controlled by Florence.

It is during these years that the Aretine valleys, and the areas surrounding them, produce the artistic innovators of the future, ranging from Masaccio from the Valdarno to Paolo Uccello from the Casentino and to Piero from the Valtiberina. At the same time, Arezzo and its territories provided noteworthy secretaries and administrators to the Florentine Republic, and subsequently to the Medici, including the humanist Leonardo Bruni, Carlo Marsuppini, Poggio Bracciolini and Benedetto Accolti. In the same years, but outside Florence, a member of the Bacci family, the future patrons of Piero, became a powerful cleric of the Camera Apostolica. Indeed, Giovanni Bacci could well have been a notable influence on the iconographic choices and the political and religious message of the frescoes of S. Francesco.

It was possibly due to the administrator, Leonardo Bruni, that the Renaissance was introduced to Arezzo through artists of a very high standard, such as the architect-sculptor Bernardo Rossellino who, in 1433, completed the upper floor of the palazzo della Fraternità dei Laici in the Piazza Grande, which was the market place and lively centre of the city. In the lunette with mixtilinear frames, which overhangs the portal, a Madonna of the Misericordia announces the advent of a new cultural era. The facade of the Fraternità dei Laici is of particular interest, not only because its completion is contemporary with Piero (apart from the Vasarian elevated terrace for the location of the clock), but also, as Marchini has shown, it contains a condensation of the many different styles found within the artistic culture of the early Renaissance at the very moment that it influences the young Piero: "From the late Gothic world of Ghiberti, Rossellino adopted the mixtilinear arch; from Donatello, the exuberant combination of plastic elements, not connected by a strict architectural logic; a hint of Michelozzi in the unadorned combination and projection of the aedicolae; from Brunelleschi, the ordered and linear arrangement of the intermediate floor, arranged in pairs of pilasters with a crowning trabeation."

The palazzo of the Fraternità dei Laici will cause us to pause a while in the Piazza Grande, which, notwithstanding its extraordinary beauty, has unfortunately lost its role as meeting point of the town. To obtain just a fleeting idea of the piazza in Piero's time, we must consider that the Logge del Vasari, constructed on its north side at the end of the sixteenth century, were an "admirable curtain dropped over the ruins of the free comune of Arezzo". Indeed, on the hill above the piazza rose the mediaeval town, destroyed by the Florentines to make way for the fortress of Sangallo. An excellent local historian, Tafi, convincingly reconstructs the situation: "In the eighteenth century, the piazza already had much of its present aspect, apart from the north side. On this side, in fact, the Vasarian logge extended well beyond the actual structure (the surface area was almost double) and were dominated, from above, by two great palazzi: on the right the Town Hall with its red tower, on the left the People's Hall with its tower. In the thirteenth century the Piazza Grande became the centre for civic activity: political, commercial, military and, at least up to the middle of the century, also religious; the Bishop had his palace between via Pescaia, Via di Seteria and the Corso and the Pieve was the most beautiful and largest church in Arezzo."

The great and innovative Florentine artistic tradition also influenced Arezzo through works of the highest quality. It

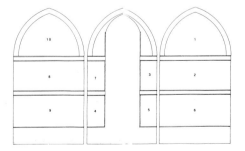

*Piero della Francesca, The Death of Adam,*
*Arezzo, Cappella Maggiore di S. Francesco.*

will suffice to mention here the *Annuncia-tion* (1436) by Beato Angelico for S. Do-menico of Cortona, at present in that city's Diocesan Museum. The predella of this work offers such a revolutionary land-scape painted from life, so tonal in its pearly distances and so convincing in its topography – the Castle of Montecchio jutting out over the swamps of the Chiana – that the hand of Piero della Francesca has been detected therein.

*Piero and the Legend of the Cross*
Piero began work on the cycle of the *Leg-end of the Cross* in about 1452. This was immediately following the death of the artist, Bicci di Lorenzo, who had been commissioned by the rich and influential family of Aretine merchants, the Bacci, to

fresco the choir of the church of S. Fran-cesco. Bicci di Lorenzo only realized the decoration of the vault and the intrados of the arch. It was, therefore, left to Piero to develop the complete narrative cycle tak-en from the *Legenda aurea* by Jacopo da Varagine or Varazze, a popular text writ-ten in the mid-thirteenth century.
Certain preliminary observations should be made concerning the subject of the fres-coes. Above all, the *Legend of the Cross* was the favourite theme of the Francis-cans; Piero would have been able to ob-serve and draw inspiration from, amongst others, the cycle by Agnolo Gaddi in S. Croce in Florence – as we have already mentioned – and that of Parri Spinelli (1387-1453) in the Badia of Arezzo, of which only a single fragment has survived,

*Piero della Francesca, The Queen of Sheba worships the Sacred Wood. Meeting with Solomon, Arezzo, Cappella Maggiore di S. Francesco.*

*Piero della Francesca, The Transport of the Sacred Wood, Arezzo, Cappella Maggiore di S. Francesco.*

*Piero della Francesca, The Annunciation,*
*Arezzo, Cappella Maggiore di S. Francesco.*

*Piero della Francesca, The Dream of
Constantine, Arezzo, Cappella Maggiore di S.
Francesco.*

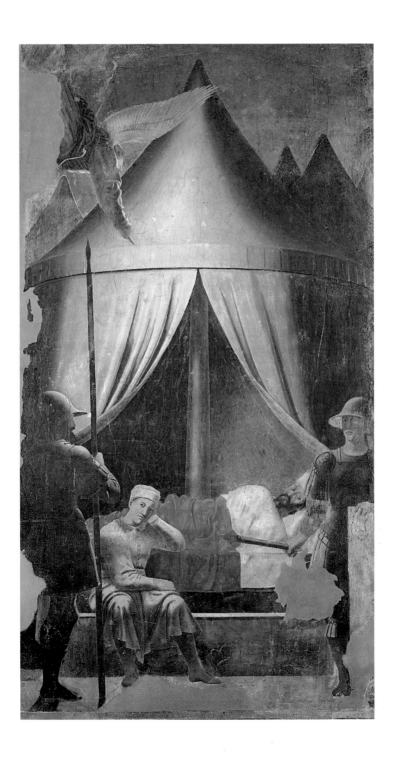

*Piero della Francesca, The Victory of*
*Constantine, Arezzo, Cappella Maggiore*
*di S. Francesco.*

now detached and conserved in the Museum of Mediaeval and Modern Art. In the mid-fifteenth century, the theme assumes unprecedented importance in ideal and programmatic terms: the exaltation of Christianity, forced to find a unity between East and West when faced with the pressure from the Islamic world, which had just caused the downfall of Constantinople (1453). This instant is perhaps connected to the emphasis placed on the two battles which take place in the lower parts of the choir, both dedicated to glorious victories over the infidel. And in this sense, we can suppose the intervention of Giovanni Bacci.

But important events in the Christian world allowed Piero to develop an extraordinary synthesis of the story of man himself from his origins to the present day, using Jacopo's structural outline. Piero's narrative projects the message of the Cross into the vivid, real world of architecture, blasons and vestments, emphasizing its saving and atemporal presence with his imperturbable and proverbial detachment and with his untiring search for a secret, and yet perceptible, order of things and events. An inheritance from both the antique and modern world, the christian message and humanist speculation are entwined in these frescoes, which contain the most complete humanist-christian synthesis.

*Narrative sequel*
Various interpretations can be given to a cycle such as the *Legend of the Cross* – it represents one of the highest moments in the history of Western figurative art. The most fitting and straightforward of these is suggested to us by the text of Jacopo da Varagine himself, but we cannot ignore the suggestive and symmetrical network of references, which connects the different scenes of the legend and has an immediate impact on the visitor. It seems to be a natural reaction to observe this network, proceeding from the bottom towards the top of the lateral walls, between one battle and another (Constantine against Maxentius, on the right; Heraclius against Chosroes, on the left), between a bipartite ceremonial scene and another with similar theme ( the meeting between the Queen of Sheba and Solomon, on the right; the discovery of the Cross, on the left), between two scenes with outdoor settings, such as those in the two facing lunettes. Even the

*Piero della Francesca, The Jew, Judas,*
*undergoes torture, Arezzo, Cappella Maggiore*
*di S. Francesco.*

*Piero della Francesca, The Discovery and Proof of the True Cross, Arezzo, Cappella Maggiore di S. Francesco.*

minor scenes are linked to one another, such as the Annunciation and the Dream of Constantine (to each side of the great window, below), connected by the motif of the angel bearing the divine message.

*The Death of Adam*
The narrative sequel of Piero actually begins with the *Death of Adam* in the large lunette on the right wall, facing the gothic window.
1. The Death of Adam. *The scene is in two parts, divided by a great tree. To the right, Adam, seated on the ground with Eve behind, announces to his descendents his imminent end. Those present, for whom the death of the old man is an incomprehensible event, listen in amazement. To the left, the dead body of Adam. His son, Set, plants in his mouth a branch of the Tree of Knowledge. Between the two scenes, in the distance Set receives the branch from the angel.*
This scene has much deteriorated with age. It is famous for the beauty of its nudes which display, for the first time in the history of modern painting, the extreme moments of vigorous youth and wizened old age. Echoes of Piero's Florentine formation include the erudite composition of the figures from Masaccio, a linearity typical of Andrea del Castagno and the physiognomic sense of Domenico Veneziano.

The re-elaboration of classic iconography, which inspired some of the figures, such as the youth leaning against a stick, can be attributed to Piero himself. No less surprising is Piero's creativity in the representation of the death throes of Adam, emphasized by the foreshortening of his figure. Simultaneously, the development of the story is further accented by the contrast between this very drastic scene of primaeval nudity and that of the most sophisticated and fashionable costume, which appears in the following scene. Before this extraordinary introduction to the *Legend of the Cross*, we recall the very pertinent comments of that lover of Italy, André Suarès, whom we have already mentioned, and who wrote the following in the twenties: "No other Florentine painting has the quality of this Legend of the Cross. Giotto is a mediaeval artist; Piero della Francesca is a painter. Leonardo is a poet absorbed in his logical, secret research, close to an intellectual mask; Piero thinks in a plastic way, with confidence and vigour. Where Masaccio has to make a great effort and is forced to rely on eloquence, Piero takes possession with serene majesty. His intellect provides a solid basis which does not collapse, not even before the imagination, typical of a poet ..... Sometimes he seems, more than any other Western painter, like a great Chinese from the antique

*Piero della Francesca, Battle of Heraclius against Chosroes.*

era. Piero paints like Tucidite and La Rochefoucald write."

*The Queen of Sheba*
2. The Queen of Sheba worships the sacred wood. The meeting of Solomon with the Queen.
*This double scene is in the middle partition on the right wall, beneath the Adamites, and represents the Queen of Sheba with her court in the act of kneeling before the wood of the future Cross and rendering homage to the wisdom of Solomon to whom she predicts the fall of the Hebrew kingdom through the sacred wood.*
These scenes presuppose other sequences from the *Legend* not featured in Piero's fresco cycle, such as the mighty growth of the Tree of Knowledge (to which an allusion is made in the preceding scene) and its felling by order of Solomon in order to construct the Temple. As it proved unsuitable for this purpose, the trunk of the tree, carved accordingly, was used as a bridge over the river Siloe.
This is the scene most frequently reproduced as an exemplary representation of courtly life in the fifteenth century. In order to give the fresco a single setting, without anulling the passage from one sequence to the other, Piero elevated the beautiful column at the corner of the portico to the role of caesura. The eye of the visitor therefore runs from left to right, from the moment of departure, represented by the grooms, to that of arrival; from outside to inside. Two different moments of the story in a calculated repetition of faces and profiles (Piero used the same cartoons and the same outlines reversed for the females figures) and in the correspondence between identical colours. Two basic qualities of the artist are emphasized in these scenes; his physiognomic realism and his pure, geometrically orientated abstraction. The male figures on one side, and the female figures on the other, embody these two qualities. The faces of the handmaidens of the Queen of Sheba are perfect examples; constructed of ovoids – two circles – one is centred on the circumference of the other. The portico of Solomon, linked proportionally to the figures and placed in severe perspective, also takes part in this subdued exaltation of geometry. It is a portico which, although of elegant renaissance design, can be related to the aedicola utilized in mediaeval works to separate a succession of narrative scenes. In this partition, Formaggio, an excellent student of Piero's chromatism, notes: "the colours are spread out in full song like a party, they are pierced with light. With startling modernity, pure white and pure black are used as colours alongside the others ... Even more surprising in

*Piero della Francesca, Heraclius returns the Cross to Jerusalem. Arezzo, Cappella Maggiore di S. Francesco.*

76

this extraordinary musical score is ... the rediscovery not only of luminous colour, that is the creation of light through colour, but the presentiment, if not the knowledge, of a totally modern method of exploiting certain laws of complimentary colours (such as red and green, for example), like that of simultaneous contrast, in which a pale green and pink juxtapositioned in equal amounts will exalt each other. One can clearly see this in the pink highlights and green shadows of the clothes of the little serving girl standing behind the group of ladies-in-waiting in the scene of the Adoration of the Wood."

As for Battisti, he realized that this famous scene contained an anticipation of cultural and social models, which were to develop

in successive centuries: "If the lunette of the Adamites aims at, and already attains, through Signorelli, a high renaissance Titanism, this delightful "city of women" is an equally fitting anticipation of Raphaelesque and mannerist idealization, which gave a dignity to woman, totally different from that late-Gothic bloodless eroticism, and, as heroine, in many cases made her equal with the men, notwithstanding her very different social position."

*The Transport of the Sacred Wood*
3. The Transport of the sacred wood.
*On the left side of the large window, above, a vertical scene with three men who remove the carved trunk of the tree to sink it in the marsh on the orders of Solomon,*

*troubled by the prophecy of the Queen of Sheba.*

With his habitual passion to provide a significance which, above and beyond literal meaning, alludes to other events, Piero used the character bearing the wood to prefigure Christ bearing the Cross. The very grain of the wood assumes the function of a halo. It is believed that this section was realized from a drawing of Piero by his collaborator, Giovanni da Piamonte, who will be mentioned again further on.

*The Annunciation*
4. The Annunciation.
*On the left of the great window, below, an angel announces the discovery of the Cross to St. Helena, mother of Constantine.*
There is no wholehearted agreement concerning the interpretation of this work, which can be seen both as part of the narrative and as an allusion to the Annunciation to Mary. The "annunciation" to St. Helena by the Eternal Father is confirmed by their presence and by the angel, who does not hold the white lily, symbol of the annunciation, but a small bamboo cross or "palmetta". Before further examination of the fresco cycle, it is worth noting that Piero omitted not only the story of the Passion, but also the account of how the wood was discovered by the Jews and transformed into the Cross. Emphasis is placed on the elegant setting of the portico in perspective, the rich hangings and the simulated tarsio, the clear light illuminating the smallest details and the harmony between the figures and the architectural elements.

*The Dream of Constantine*
5. The Dream of Constantine
*In the section to the right of the great window, below, Constantine, three hundred years later, is visited by an angel, who announces in a dream his victory over Maxentius, in the form of a cross.*
This very famous nocturnal scene, rendered even more atmospheric by the artificial illumination, used in an intense but efficient way to emphasize the outlines of the figures with its own golden dust. The

light which seeps into the tent, in which Constantine sleeps, alludes to the enlightening message of the angel. The effects of the illumination are balanced once again by the taste for geometric abstraction, which appears in the perfect cone of the tent, in the modular repetition of this form and in the symmetrical harmony between the raised curtain and the soldiers.

*The Victory of Constantine over Maxentius*
6. The victory of Constantine over Maxentius.
*Comforted by the nocturnal visit of the angel, Constantine, bearing the symbol of the cross, forces Maxentius into retreat.*
This scene is traditionally considered the most evocative of the entire cycle of S. Francesco. An unprecedented polyphonic dimension establishes a series of different vocabularies: the fantastic world of chivalry and heraldry, bristling with lances, armour and banners; the intense yet composed drama of the victory itself; the clear river landscape; the intense and uniform daylight; the figures of the men and horses which scan the space and assert their own terse forms even in the details. "The hooves of the horses, soft as slippers, make before them a feint shadow", to cite an effective description by Longhi. The scene is set by Piero in his native Valtiberina, at the first sinuous bend of the Tiber, as though he wished to accentuate the new course that history would take after this event. As always, Piero's valley rises, an ideal microcosm in which the events of the wider universe are reflected in a clear epitome (and hence, the single and unmistakeable reason for the itinerary in search of Piero).
The river in perspective also has the function of dividing the scene into two parts: to the left, the parade of Constantine's army, moving parallel to the wall, and the foreshortened white horse, springing forward at a slant and thus providing the illusion of a deep, wide curve; to the right, the retreat of Maxentius (today seriously damaged) caused by the collapse of a bridge, so that, as the *Legenda aurea* relates, "the hands of Constantine were not stained with blood."

"The posture of the horses reminds us of the paintings and medals of Pisanello", noted Sir James Dennistoun more than a century ago, a then rare admirer of Piero. Pisanello also inspired the portrait of Constantine by Piero with its strange oriental headgear. And since the medal by Pisanello represents the Emperor of the East, Giovanni VIII Paleologo, champion of the union of the churches, it is just as likely that the scene is also linked to contemporary events: the fall of Constantinople to the Turks, the counter-attack of the beseiged christians, the promulgation of a crusade against the infidel.

This scene is one of the most praised by foreign visitors. Amongst the many testimonies left to us, that written by Otto Braun in 1913 is particularly interesting: "Piero's composition and sense of colour also reach an astounding level of perfection. The figures of Constantine and Maxentius are beautiful .....Constantine stretches out his pale thin hand, in such a way that the cross he is holding, surrounded by a soft luminosity, almost becomes the meeting point of all the lines; whilst Maxentius turns in anguish to one side, the horse, in admirable contrast, drags himself out of the ditch on the other. Constantine himself gazes full of tranquil confidence at the sacred wood. The bulwark of spears behind the Emperor provides a background against which his figure stands out in potent relief, acquiring thus greater importance than that given to Maxentius, who is left alone, in a warlike tumult, the daring and ingenious conception of which astounds; one can only compare this with the Surrender of the Breda by Velasquez and perhaps also the Battle of Alexander."

*The torture of the Jew, Judas.*
7. To the left of the great window, above, the Jew, Judas, undergoes interrogation and torture.
*Having become Emperor, Constantine sends St. Helena, his mother, to the Holy Land in search of the crosses of Golgotha, buried after the death of Christ.*
*Helena tortures the Jew, Judas, the only one capable of revealing their location, by lowering him for seven days "into a dry well and leaving him there to starve".*

Even though this scene is attributed to Piero's collaborator, Giovanni da Piamonte, as demonstrated by the dull rather than imperturbed expressions of the characters, the scene has a remarkable originality. From a point of view of the composition, this is due to its position in the pyramidal space of the wooden framework supporting Judah. No less effectively alienating is the modernity of the judicial proceedings, as though the judge interrogating the tortured were carrying out legal action in the cerimonial hall of a renaissance court. With this in mind, one observes the architectural wing on the left and the crenellated wall at the back. As Battisti has remarked, "the weary emergence of the tortured", together with the wooden framework, anticipate "both figuratively and iconographically the discovery of the crosses and the resurrection of the dead youth", depicted in the large middle section to the left, which follows this scene in the narrative sequence.

*The Discovery of the Cross*
8. The Discovery and Proof of the True Cross.
*Wall to the left of the choir, middle section. The scene which faces the meeting of the Queen of Sheba with Solomon, is divided into two parts with symmetrical cross-references. On the left, Judas arranges the disinterment of the three crosses, buried at the gate of Jerusalem under the Temple of Venus in the presence of St. Helena, courtiers and diggers. On the right, the revelation of the True Cross through the raising up of a dead boy from his bier.*

The two scenes are marked by a typically urban setting. The discovery of the crosses is set against a synthetic view of the city of Arezzo, which substitutes Jerusalem. This has been compared with an identical view by Giotto in Assisi, figuring S. Francesco chasing the devils out of the city of Arezzo, and the contemporary view in the background of the already mentioned Deposition by Angelico in S. Marco, in Florence. Longhi also perceived "the structure of certain villages in Provence immortalized by Cezanne." The proof of the True Cross, on the other hand, takes place within an urban context, before a temple inspired by Alberti, the Temple of the Legenda aurea. The foreshortened row of palaces on the extreme right is, however, an homage by Piero to San Sepolcro and represents the actual via Buia with the pyramidal cusped bell tower of the Camaldolese Badia, the present cathedral. As a whole, the urban space depicted by Piero seems to be an elegant Albertian development of Masaccio's interpretation of space in the frescoes of the Brancacci chapel.

At the architectural division of the scenes, a circle of figures are positioned before the two miraculous events, thus suggesting a three-dimensional space in syntony with the perspective of the landscape to the left and the town street to the right. We have already emphasized the sense of continuity of this scene with the preceding vertical one, due to the figures lifting themselves or emerging from the ground. We should not forget the implicit specular link between this great divided image and that facing it, which illustrates the meeting of Solomon with the Queen of Sheba. Both, in fact, are ritual, courtly scenes, made noble by the courtly/aulic economy of gesture and the important role of the architecture, even though St. Helena, in the scene depicting the disinterment of the crosses, wears the humble cloak of a pilgrim and the well-made clothes of the diggers appear disshevelled. The unusual anatomy of the youth rising up from the bier is of particular interest – his structure foreshortened in order to increase the sense of depth – due to the pictorial plastic sensitivity used in the depiction of his back turned towards the observer.

*The Battle of Heraclius*
9. To the left, below, the battle of the Emperor of the East, Heraclius, against Chosroes; the defeat and decapitation of Chosroes.
*The Emperor Heraclius, having assembled his troups, fights against the son of Chosroes, King of Persia. At the height of the battle, with a presentiment of his defeat, the old Chosroes kneels beneath the canopy of his throne to await his decapitation.*
For a complete understanding of this

scene, we must remember that the battle presupposes events which took place three hundred years after the recovery of the cross by St. Helena. The Persian King Chosroes, having reached Jerusalem in his conquest of the world, was frightened by the tomb of Christ and decided to take the true Cross with him. Having left his kingdom to his son, he was overcome with a mania of greatness and he insisted that his people worship him. He called himself – as the *Legenda* notes – "Domeneddio" and remained permanently seated on the throne with the Cross on his right, in place of the Son, and a cock on his left, in place of the Holy Spirit. Both symbols delimit the canopy which hangs above the humiliated Chosroes.

It seems more than natural to make a comparison between the two scenes of battle which face each other on the walls of the choir. This reveals that in contrast to the triumphal, unwarlike parade of Constantine and quite distinctly from the retreat of Maxentius, the battle between Heraclius and Chosroes and his son presents neither solutions of continuity nor distinctions between the victorious and the defeated. The whole wall provides a sense of a well-calculated confusion "of wounded, fallen and dead" – as Vasari comments. This is increased by the complete absence of foreshortening and of elements placed at a slant to suggest three dimensional depth and space. It is not by chance that the effect of compact narrative continuity in this scene has often been related to classical bas-reliefs or to decorated Roman columns. Furthermore, Piero makes up for the sense of depth by raising the figures in the background on an artificial base; indeed if these were to be placed on the same level as the figures in the foreground, they would even exceed the horses in height. This scene has often been compared with the *Battle of S. Romano* by Paolo Uccello – which we have already seen in the Uffizi – noted for its fairy tale atmosphere created by the visual fragmentation which the rigorous and abstract perspective study of the single elements produces on the overall effect of the scene. As Nicco Fasola wrote, Piero, in contrast to

*Parri Spinelli, Maxentius in flight, Arezzo,
Museum of Medieval and Modern Art.*

*View of S. Maria della Pieve, from A. Terreni,
Viaggio pittorico della Toscana.*

*View of the amphitheatre of Arezzo.*

this, did not consider perspective either as an absolute or a single system, but as "one of the factors of invention, subject like the others to variations imposed by fantastic elaboration according to the prevalence or the moderation or the mutual emphasis of the expressive elements."

It is believed that the characters surrounding the kneeling Chosroes are portraits of the patrons and sponsors of the cycle.

*Heraclius returns the True Cross*
10. Great lunette to the left: Heraclius returns the True Cross to Jerusalem.
*Surrounded by dignitaries, the Emperor Heraclius, barefooted and in the act of repentance, approaches the walls of Jerusalem. On the right of the scene, under the powerful crennellated walls of the city, a group of citizens prepare to worship the Cross.*

This is the final scene of the entire cycle which Piero drew with liberal invention from the *Legenda aurea* by Jacopo da Varagine. The division of the scene, suggested by the wide space between the two groups of figures, does not correspond, as in the other scenes, to different moments in the story. This has reached its own unequivocal outcome. The lack of originality and the weakened expressive force of this scene has often been noted, in particular in comparison with the lunette representing the Adamites facing it and with which the narrative begins. And yet this scene of quiet adoration leads the fresco cycle, which began with the incredulity of the first men before the sudden arrival of death, into the ritual solemnity of rediscovered human serenity in the form of the Cross. Few but fundamental devices render the scene original, such as the oriental hat of Heraclius, which raises him above the other figures, and the empty space before the Cross which increase the sacred and celebrative quality of the scene. We thus conclude the epic story of strong men, in action and in meditation, in whose presence we have learnt to be enchanted by light and colour and to study human thought using the numerical rules of the universe.

*Parri Spinelli, Madonna della Misericordia,*
*Arezzo, Museum of Mediaeval and Modern Art.*

*Diligence in front of S. Maria della Pieve,
XIXth century lithograph*

*View of Arezzo from beyond the Porta S.
Spirito, 1830.*

*Pupils and followers of Piero*
Apart from the scenes described, Piero and
his collaborators, Giovanni da Piamonte
and Lorentino d'Andrea, were responsible
for figures such as the two *Prophets*, which
are to be found on the apse wall, to the
right and to the left of the great window.
The prophet to the right is attributed to
Piero. Completing the iconographical and
decorative plan of Bicci di Lorenzo, two
doctors of the Church, *Sant'Agostino* and
*Sant'Ambrogio*, within the intrados of the
triumphal arch, attributed to Giovanni da
Piamonte, a *Cupid* in the act of hurling an
arrow in the chapel pilaster of access and
the head of an *Angel* in the intrados of the
right pilaster.

*In Search of Piero*
We have already mentioned that a journey
in search of Piero implies, above all in an
age of rapid travel, a certain amount of the
ancient magic of the *quête*, of empassioned
and marvelling research. Many have
sensed this suggestive quality in the loca-
tions set aside for his works. Here in Arezzo, however, the sense of the dazzling
discovery, capable of revealing one of the
highest moments in the figurative tradition
to the visitor, finds its origins in another,
more dramatic order of events which we
can neither forget, nor fail to notice.
Before the splendid colours of Piero, before this chromatic exaltion of bodies,
clothing, simulated marbles, landscapes,
before the "pure streams and clear skies"
with which d'Annunzio summarized the
sense of wonder of the first, unsuspecting
visitors, the modern student cannot ignore
the fact that Piero is perhaps the most
misunderstood and damaged artist in five
centuries of civilization. Not more than
fifty years after his death, entire cycles of
his frescoes in Ferrara and in the Palazzo
Vaticano in Rome were already being chi-
selled away to make room for other artists'
work; and not long afterwards many of his
works disappeared from S. Ciriaco di Ancona, Pesaro, Rimini and Loreto, not to mention the works in his native country, in
Arezzo and in San Sepolcro. The misfor-
tunes which befell the *Legend of the Cross*
have already been mentioned.

Important evidence of this oversight, if not
grave negligence, of history – perhaps
made uncomfortable by the impeturbility
of Piero della Francesca – is the absence of
a critical history of Piero and his works,
which could serve the student and admirer. On the other hand, the visitor to the
frescoes of S. Francesco is subjected to yet
another anxiety on each visit; anxiety for
their future. He knows that this extraordinary synthesis of form and colour is gradually fading, as though infected by a mysterious anaemia. It is difficult to say at the
moment if the analyses and remedies studied by the "Project for Piero della Francesca" will succeed in conserving the intensi-
ty and chromatic delicacy of the most
beautiful frescoed choir in existence or if
modern research is capable of rendering
the discovery of Piero and his recent re-
emergence from the shadows of negligence
less ephimeral.

We cannot, therefore, take leave of these
frescoes without recalling a very recent
and singularly allusive page written by
John Mortimer in 1988: "Although she had
done her best to prepare herself for Arezzo, Molly still had difficulty in making out
the story. Things were not made easier by
the fact that the frescoes were only illuminated when someone put money into a
machine, and so were often plunged into
sudden darkness, like Hugh's old bedsitter
when the meter ran out. In many places
the paint had faded, leaving naked stretches of wall, blotting out half a battle, the
legs of a torturer or a woman's face. Then,
as the lights came on and the walls were lit
up with sky blue and stone grey, the green
of grapes and olives, the pale red of wine
held up to the light, she saw the round,
invariably handsome, always unsmiling
faces, with eyelids that seemed heavy as
stone, looking down with perpetual detachment and even, in the case of the
women, a kind of contempt."

*Aretine art related to Piero*
The visitor who can concede more time to
the city of Arezzo and its immediate surroundings, which we will leave to the excellent local guidebooks, will find many
artistic references related to Piero della

84

*Bartolomeo della Gatta, S. Rocco chases the Plague from Arezzo, Arezzo, Museum of Mediaeval and Modern Art.*

Francesca. These appear as a thematic anticipation of certain examples of his own work and a result of a more or less direct diffusion of his non too easy teaching. We are now dealing with works both of a high artistic quality and of quite humble idea and realization, but which are capable of rendering the "meteor" of Piero less isolated and peremptory. The church of S. Francesco, where we found the *Legend of the Cross*, also houses paintings by a collaborator of Piero, Lorentino d'Arezzo, or d'Andrea, who frescoed the *Crucifix* in the Carbonati Chapel (1463), which is almost a copy of that which Piero painted as a cusp to the polyptych of the *Misericordia* of Borgo San Sepolcro. Lorentino also attempted a *Madonna of the Misericordia*; this is in S. Francesco, where he also painted the chapel of S. Antonio with anecdotal stories, almost an *ex-voto*, of the saint.

Not far from here, the original Romanesque Pieve of S. Maria, with its perforated bell-tower, "a great flute with rectangular facades", as Suarès said, houses the majestic *Polyptych of the Madonna with Child and Saints* by Pietro Lorenzetti on the main altar. Piero would have definitely seen this work; the finest example of fourteenth century Sienese painting on Aretine soil.

Works of particular interest, which help us to understand, at least in general terms, the contemporary Aretine artistic scene, are in the Museum of Mediaeval and Modern Art. The visitor will not fail to observe the most elegant and ornamental version of the Madonna of the Misericordia to be found in this area. It is the *Madonna della Misericordia with Saints Lorentino and Pergentino* by Parri Spinelli, or Parri di Spinello and dates to 1437. We should remember this painting, together with other versions of the same subject present in this museum, when we visit the *Madonna della Misericordia* by Piero della Francesca in San Sepolcro.

Another work by Parri Spinello is also extremely interesting. It is a fragment of detached monochrome fresco representing the *Defeat of Maxentius*, which formed part of the lost cycle of the Badia. The central figure of the fleeing knight, who turns to look behind him, is copied with total fidelity from Piero's version of the same battle in the choir of S. Francesco.

Local artists of great talent and originality include the Camaldolese Pietro Dei, known as Bartolomeo della Gatta (1448-1502), represented by two works, *St. Rocco driving the plague from Arezzo* and *St. Rocco before the Palazzo della Fraternità dei Laici*. It has in fact been observed by A.M. Maetzke that "the meeting with Piero della Francesca must have exercised a profound and maturing influence on his painting .... even though he was probably never an actual pupil of Piero, he became the most direct and ingenious heir." To become aware of this genius, it is enough to visit the Diocesan Museum with the extraordinary S. Gerolamo and, a few kilometres from Arezzo, *The Stigmata of St. Francis*, in the Civic Pinacoteca of Castiglion Fiorentino (Clark's drawing teacher advised his young student to study this work), and in S. Domenico in Cortona, the *Altar-piece of the Assumption*. But once again we must remember not to wander too far from our route.

With the risk of repetition, we should recall that this is a guide in search of Piero in his native land. We wish, therefore, to point out more specific and recent guides, from Martelli to Nibbi, and excellent historic and artistic reconstructions of the city, from Tafi to Salmi, and many others mentioned in the bibliography, for those who intend to visit the whole of Arezzo. This city, in its historic stratification, its wealth of museums and the range and quality of the artistic heritage of its surroundings is still worthy of discovery.

*Santa Maria delle Grazie*

At the edge of the city, not far from the turning for San Sepolcro, we find the monumental complex of S. Maria delle Grazie which, amongst its many visitors, enchanted Virginia Woolf. The integration of the fourteenth century monastery and church with the area of the loggia and the vast quadrangular portico, which originally bordered the wide space used for a market, makes the complex "the first example of a porticoed Renaissance piazza", as Salmi writes. The loggia in front of the church, erected by Benedetto da Maiano between 1478 and 1482 is particularly evocative. The seven arches receive impetus from the high "pulvini" and the sharp caesure of the abaci, whereas the lateral arches offer a harmoniously organic view of the complex, complete in itself. The arcade, work of Giuliano da Maiano, of which only two parts survive, was demolished at the end of the seventeenth century. We will stop by this monument because, apart from it being one of the finest examples of Renaissance art, the first *Madonna della Misericordia*, in chronological order, painted by Parri Spinelli can be found above the main altar. This seems an excellent viaticum to go and see the *Madonna della Misericordia* by Piero. Thinking about refreshment before our departure, the words of Louis Simonin, geologist and estruscologist, come to mind; he stayed in Arezzo in 1865, and left an unparalleled description of an Aretine inn: "On my arrival in Arezzo, my first thought was for a guide and an hotel. For the latter, I was directed to the 'Tamburro', an ancient inn which had apparently welcomed Michelangelo and Vasari, being three centuries old. Throughout the centuries it has remained the property of the same family. Old enamelled plates from Faenza hang upon the blackened walls of the kitchen. On the stairs there is an old painting of the Madonna in Byzantine style, protected by glass, before which a candle has burned for more than three hundred years."

We have already mentioned Castiglion Fiorentino and Cortona in relation to artistic masterpieces from Beato Angelico to Bartolomeo della Gatta, which accentuate the wealth of the Aretine artistic scene at the time of Piero and are therefore related to his influence. A visit to these cities, steeped in Aretine history on the beautiful hilly side of the Valdichiana, would be to wander from our itinerary of Piero della Francesca. In any case, we point them out as a destination for further travels through Aretine land.

## From Arezzo to Monterchi
## and San Sepolcro

*Journey from Arezzo to San Sepolcro and Sestino, from Guida per viaggiar la Toscana, XVIIIth century.*

*J. Furttenbach, Map of the Itinerary of Italy, with the route from Florence to Ancona, from Newes Itinerarium Italiae, 1627.*

*"There are very few things more lovely in the world than the upper valley of the Arno, but one of them is, I think, the upper valley of the Tiber.*
*It is a landscape more virile than Umbria – a landscape by Piero della Francesca."*
Edward Hutton

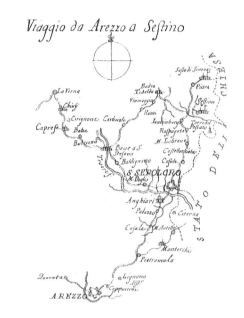

*Two Possible Routes*
A journey from Arezzo to San Sepolcro – the "miniscule city", native town of Piero della Francesca – leads us into a landscape of natural and evocative beauty which reveals, along the way, views painted by its most famous artist on the walls of S. Francesco and on the panels, long ago removed from his native land. Indeed Piero maintained a continuous relationship with his city, to which he returned whenever possible, and was involved not only in artistic activities, which would be natural, but also in the public administration and the family commercial business. Battisti wrote with sensitivity upon this permanent vocation, unusual in an artist: "It is not by chance that the continual backdrop for the painting of Piero is the walled city of Borgo Sansepolcro, which he himself helped to consolidate, or its calm valley, crossed by rivers near to their sources, cut by straight roads of communication and closed in by mountains of delicate and precise profile. The artist, whose nature was devoid of drama, never seems to have wished to leave this background and this climate, either in his imagination or physically. He never agreed on a prolonged stay far from his city in the continuous service of a distant court."

His is an implicit, singular and in some aspects, unexpected, case which transforms our journey towards Piero's valley once again into a pilgrimage.
A journey to San Sepolcro signifies, therefore, perceiving in the landscape itself the prolonged relationship of Piero with his native land and, by means of that silent affair, an important aspect of his art. For the modern traveller and tourist, it also signifies exploring an ancient route at an unusually slow pace. Between Arezzo and Piero's city, in fact, there is the important

*Romayne Robert, View of Arezzo and Anghiari, travel note-book, circa 1896.*

AREZZO

ANGHIARI

road which connected Tuscany to the Adriatic, from Florence to Ancona. One need only remember the words of Montaigne in his *Voyage d'Italie*, or those of Furttenbach, which note the stages and inns at Chaveretto and Anghiari after Arezzo in a route which today corresponds in large part to the S.P. 43 della Libbia.

We will take, however, the Statale 73 for San Sepolcro, which permits us to stop at Monterchi. It is a road that was discovered – so to speak – with the unification of Italy and leads from Umbria into the upper valley of the Tiber.

In both cases, we are dealing with roads which keep an old-fashioned way of travelling alive. As Ruskin wrote, "when, from the top of the last hill he had surmounted, the traveller beheld the quiet village where he was to rest". The meandering roads seem made to slow the traveller down and force him into a less fleeting and ephimeral relationship with the surrounding landscape. These are roads which seem, paradoxically, to confirm William Blake's motto that progress makes a straight path but the ways of the genius are tortuous.

*The Valley of the Cerfone*
For Monterchi and San Sepolcro, we follow the Statale 73, which the Anglo-Florentine, Thomas Adolphus Trollope, suggested to nineteenth century tourists – we are in 1860 – who wished to deviate from the usual itinerary of the Grand Tour. We shall take Trollope as our guide from here almost to the door of the chapel of the cemetry of Monterchi, journeying through space and time, imagining his experiences and reconsidering his picturesque reflections on the "modern" method of travelling. Apart from the first part of the route, which crosses the Scopettone near to Torrino and can be achieved with some speed, the itinerary followed by Trollope along the unchanged and secluded valley of the Cerfone does not appear very different.

Let us listen, therefore, to our guide: "We – I and my companion, that is to say – went forth from Arezzo by a far less used gate directly facing the mountains, which, as soon as we had crossed the small extent of flat and fertile fields lying around the knoll crowned by the city, we began at once to climb.

They are outlying spurs of the Apennines....Here and there was a bleak and
dreary looking farm-house, with its usual
dove-cot on the top of it, and a half-dozen
or so of doves painted on the white walls
around the pigeon-holes, for the purpose, I
suppose, of showing the real birds the way
in. It seemed difficult to imagine what
business farm-houses could have in such
situations, till a more minute examination
of the surrounding hill-sides discovered
here and there a few isolated patches of
painfully cultivated and ungrateful soil,
which constituted the mountain farm.

And the specimens of the population of
this hill country, who were coming down
to the city as we were climbing the hill,
and leaving it behind us, seemed quite in
character with the physiognomy of their
country. A young priest, who could hardly
have been guessed to be such, save for the
indispensable little linen collar, which had
sometime towards the early part of the
current year been white, came trudging
down the hillside brandishing a stout cud-
gel as he walked. He was dressed in a
ragged and threadbare blue cloth coat,
which came down to his heels, and a sadly
battered and shapeless chimney-pot hat;
he had a stubble black beard a week old,
and a lean, hungry, gaunt look, which told
the poverty- stricken state of his cure
among these barren hills, more eloquently
that aught else could have done. What
must the poverty of the flock be when
such was the shepherd!

Then at the next turn of the winding road,
came a solitary charcoal-burner, with his
half-score of black sacks closed at the
mouth with twigs of arbutus, laden on a
very miserable-looking, lean little pony,
whose meek head peered out from beneath
his overhanging load. Charcoal-burners
share by prescription the picturesqueness
of brigands ...."

After these sketchy notes, usual by this
time in travel literature, Trollope once
again takes up the description of the route:
"the ridge we were crossing forms the
watershed between the valley of the Arno
and that of the *Tiber*. We were therefore
when we passed it, still on the Tuscan side
of the main chain of the Apennines. But

*Piero della Francesca, Madonna del Parto,
detail.*

the style of scenery is entirely different. A steep descent brought us down to the margin of a rapid stream, which finds its winding way through a series of wooded gorges to the Tiber. Cerfone is its name; and it deserves to be mentioned by it; for the combinations of rock, wood, water, and mountain, through which the road winds as it follows the banks of the stream, passing once or twice beneath the grey ruins of a mediaeval fortress tower, would have been cited ere now as equal to much of the vaunted scenery of the Moselle, if they had not laboured under the same disadvantage as the heroes who lived before Agamemnon, and died unpraised, *"caruerunt quia vate sacro"*.
Following this panegyrical reference to the late-Roman poet, Ausonius, Trollope continues towards our goal: "The route follows this charming valley of the Cerfone till it opens into the wide basin of the Tiber, about seven miles above Città di Castello.
Just at the opening of the smaller valley into that of the Tiber there is a singularly situated isolated knoll, with the little walled town of Monterchi on its summit.
The road winds round this rising ground, closely skirting its base, before it takes its course down the valley of the Tiber; and thus gives the traveller a series of views of this strikingly picturesque little hill-town, seen from different sides, and with varied

backgrounds."
The itinerary revealed by Trollope to the new flocks of post-unification tourists was to become an increasingly popular route to reach these prophetic places of Piero; an itinerary which was to gain more popularity by the inauguration of a railway line following its sinuous path to the Valtiberina.
Dismantled definitively after the Second World War, the central railway of Umbria was remembered in the travelling literature of the first part of the twentieth century, thanks to its "small low comedy railway", as it was defined by Aldous Huxley, and its "American" carriages with their central corridors, as Williams remarked.

*The Pieve at Ranco*
Before reaching Le Ville and the short deviation leading to Monterchi, it is pleasant to stop for a few minutes at Ranco and enter the Pieve of SS. Lorentino and Pergentino. There is a fifteenth century polychrome wooden statue on the high altar of the church, which seems vaguely inspired by the female figures of Piero with the sophisticated elegance of their hairstyles.
Before this Madonna, not devoid of her own reserved worldliness, we notice how the influence of Piero della Francesca and the impeccable and courtly taste which constitutes each one of his figures are scattered throughout these valleys, finding an echo of elegant, but sensitive and talented, ingenuity in this unknown artist.

*The View of Monterchi*
Amongst the recent descriptions of this route, Lucy Lilian Notestein wrote in 1963: "There is one pilgrimage, however, that any visitor to Arezzo will wish to make, to see two great paintings of Piero, one at Monterchi, the other at Sansepolcro. We set out on a misty morning and were soon climbing the first range to the east, winding among hills clothed with spruces and with hardwoods just turning from green to yellow and to red. The dampness made the coloration seem more intense; one might have thought oneself among the Pennsylvania hills.

Up the valley of the Torrente Cerfone we finally saw to our right, on the crest of a steep hill, the village of Monterchi. We were not bound there, though it looked inviting, but rather to its *campo santo* (cemetery) a little farther on and up a long lane to the left." A few years before this, one of the last of the "old fashioned" travellers to Italy stopped for a long time in the village of Monterchi: in his travel book of 1957, H.V. Morton recalls: "In a maze of side-roads that twist in all directions three or four miles west of the young Tiber, a hill covered with the white, red roofed buildings of a small town rises from the plain. Its name is Monterchi, which is the modern corruption of *Mons Herculis*; and it was the birthplace of Piero's mother. The view from its ramparts is magnificent.

I looked north across the Tiber valley to the Alpe della Luna and south into Umbria. It was wonderful to stand there on a summer's morning and to follow the white threads of the lanes between the vineyards and the orchards, and to hear, borne up upon the hot and lazy air, such country sounds as the barking of farm dogs, the song of an invisible worker in the fields, and the creak of an ox-wagon as it wound its way round the hill up to the quiet, pretty little town.

On the flat land at the foot of Monterchi a double line of cypress trees leads up to the cemetery on the hillside opposite the town, and in its tiny mortuary chapel Piero della Francesca painted one of his most famous frescoes – *Madonna del Parto* – the Pregnant Madonna."

*The Madonna del Parto*

We are now in the presence of one of the most remarkable works by Piero and in the Italian figurative tradition; for it seems impossible to find another example of an "expectant Madonna". The visitor's sense of isolation and of discovery caused by this painting is superbly expressed by Clark, who writes that the *Madonna del Parto* "is one of the few great works of art which are still relatively inaccessible, and to visit it offers some of the pleasures of a pilgrimage.

Only after much wanderings and misdirec-

tion do we reach a rustic cemetery on a hill a few miles outside the village of Monterchi, where the custodian seems to understand the nature of our quest; and it is with scepticism and apprehension that we see her open the doors to a tiny graveyard chapel.

In this heightened state of perception we are suddenly confronted with the splendid presence of the Madonna, rising up, "full without boast", only a few feet away from us. That this effect, as of a sudden revelation, was in Piero's mind, is evident from the device of the two angels pulling back a curtain".

The *Madonna del Parto* is depicted in the act of indicating the fruit of the conception with her right hand. We stand before the exaltation of humanity and, simultaneously, the regality of the Virgin. She is, in fact, almost with didactic clarity, a tabernacle of the living God and instrument of salvation for mankind. Placed in the centre of a regal pavilion – indicated by the ermine lining – which plays the role of a temple, the Madonna is turned just enough to reveal her swollen stomach. The two angels, taken from the same cartoon, lift the edges of the curtain in perfect symmetry and confer upon her even greater importance due to the noticeable difference in their dimensions.

We also discover that the *Madonna del Parto* maintains unaltered its own evocative nature, thus providing the itinerary with a hint of the true pilgrimage. In its singular, modern simplicity, in its disarmingly natural evocation of the turgid swelling of the seed of life in the field of death, the *Madonna del Parto* permits a glimpse of archaic roots, which have fascinated critics and travellers. Tradition has it that the Madonna, related to the place of birth of the artist's mother, and beyond that to a place of confirmed galactic cult, has powers which, even in a literary connotation, produce the effective agitation of the viewer as though an ancient idol, an idol into which has been condensed a remote religious piety. Such is the meaning of the "tiny mountain facing the charcoal burner's door" of Longhi and such, with even more reason, the reference of Clark to the

*View of Monterchi, from A. Terreni, Viaggio pittorico della Toscana.*

*J. Pennell, View of the Upper Valley of Tiber, circa 1899, Florence, Uffizi.*

*Piero della Francesca, The Victory of Constantine, detail with the Tiber.*

detachment of a great sculpture of Buddha. The latter is a happy intuition, perhaps inspired by the downward cast of the slanting eyes between sinuous almond-shaped eyelids, which projects the *Madonna del Parto* into a dimension of myth, beyond memory.

"When people come to see me", noted Muriel Spark recently, "I usually take them to see the majestic Madonna del Parto of Piero della Francesca. This fresco is to be found entirely on its own, in a small cemetery chapel at Monterchi. Peasant-like and noble, the picture is planned to represent a stage, the Virgin herself both dramatic protagonist and actual theatre, as she opens her dress to prepare for the historic curtain rise of the Incarnation".

What better synthesis could be offered by a cultured and sensitive traveller to other fervent pilgrims?

*Citerna*

Before returning over a small tract of the S.P. 221 towards le Ville and from there, to San Sepolcro, the visitor with half an hour to spare, can climb the hill overlooking the cemetry – following the signposts *in loco* – to visit the mediaeval town of Citerna.

From the walled city there is an incomparable view over the upper valley of the Tiber, wide and perfectly contained, spread out before the observer in a range of colours, typical of Piero della Francesca. With his usual British sense of topography, the famous historian Trevelyan notes: "This reach of the great river, where it first leaves its mountain cradle, has a peculiar effect on the imagination, for the valley, several miles broad, through which it flows, combines the freshness of an Alp with the wealth and spaciousness of a populous countryside, and through the thick web of vines that nets the plain runs the line of poplar woods shading the course of the Tiber, a clear stream of blue and silver eddies".

*Anghiari*

Returning from Citerna or from Monterchi on the Statale 73, in a very short time one reaches the top of a soft ridge of hills, with earth the colour of rust, and the turning

*Piero della Francesca, Madonna del Parto,*
*Monterchi, Cemetery Chapel.*

*View of Anghiari.*

*A. Terreni, View of Borgo San Sepolcro.*

*Anton Maria Lancisi, Captaincy and lands of Borgo San Sepolcro, 1731, Florence, Archivio di Stato.*

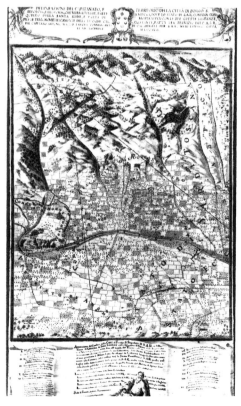

for Anghiari. Once again, our traveller may proceed directly as the crow flies along the Statale 73 towards Piero's native city, or otherwise, make a short deviation towards the intact mediaeval town of Anghiari (S.P. 47 of Caprese Michelangelo).

This city is worthy of an unhurried visit, particularly as the traveller can then continue along the Provinciale 43 – Montaigne's road – which leads to San Sepolcro; a straight stretch of road almost unchanged since Piero's time. Indeed, so unchanged that it has been identified in a youthful work of Piero, the *Baptism of Christ*, once in the Cathedral of San Sepolcro, sold in 1860 by the chapter to an emissary of the British government and now in the National Gallery of London. The dewy valley, the humped hills behind, the clear and twisty river, the rich and varied flora, and the fortified town in the painting can easily be identified as the upper valley of the Tiber. The town in the painting is reached by a straight road, leading from the river, which is in fact the last part of the road to Anghiari, and is that which we still see today from the top of Anghiari cutting straight across the valley. Between the sixteenth and seventeenth centuries this road was noted with implicit curiosity in the *Guide* by Joseph Furttenbach: "We continued on our journey ...to Borgo San Sepolcro. Before the inn for three miles there is a flat, straight road which provides a beautiful view overlooking the city. This is quite large with an elevated fortress and belongs, like all of the land we have so far crossed, to the Granduchy of Tuscany."

The external circuit of the walls of Anghiari reveals an enchanting view over a wide radius of the upper valley of the Tiber.

For the traveller who wishes to deviate, other "Piero della Francesca" views are spread out before him at the first bend in the road from Anghiari to Caprese Michelangelo.

The most effective synthesis of this memorable fusion between real landscape and that painted in the background of the *Baptism*, of the *San Gerolamo* in the Galleria dell'Accademia and of the *Resurrection*, has been beautifully written by Leslie Gar-

*Map of the Valtiberina, XVIIth century. The roads are marked between San Sepolcro and Anghiari (A), Citerna (C), Badia S. Veriano (F), Montauto (N), Florence, Archivio di Stato.*

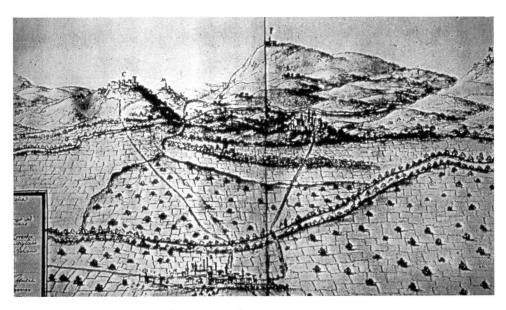

diner, whom we have already mentioned, but whose words we transcribe here in their entirety. Since their publication in 1971 to today, their author's affectionately ironic, arcadian image has disappeared, inexorably changed: "No man, Herodotus says, bathes twice in the same river. Certainly the Tiber is different after thirty years, or my view of it is different. It used to be a flashing stream, blue and silver. The colours along its course were strong: the chalky boulders in the summer bed whiter than white, the marsh-flowers of the shallows more yellow than gold. The river was thrown like a necklace round the mills and ruined abbeys and those hump-backed, fortress-crowned hillocks which had strayed out of the green forest. Those were my recollections, but perhaps I have confused personal memories with the Tiber that Piero della Francesca depicted, the sky reflecting rivulet along whose banks a farm hand drives a flock of geese – a distracting *pastorale* for the poor cavalry horse in that painter's "Legend of the Cross", who turns aside to drink."

Before leaving Anghiari, let us at least suggest, in connection with Piero della Francesca, a visit to the polyptych of Matteo di Giovanni in the church of Sant'Agos-

tino. Anghiari, as a whole, represents an intact example of a mediaeval town; its houses are constructed on very narrow streets which close in a spiral around the Town Hall on top of the hill on which the town is built. It is also worth noting briefly that apart from the admirable defensive arrangement of the buildings, the originality of the facades of the houses, the portals, the pavements, the beaten iron and the carvings contribute to the exceptional value of this historic and artistic town. But, as we have already mentioned, such a varied and even today, unspoilt place, is worthy of a proper visit.

Descending into the valley, shortly after having taken the large road which runs directly towards the Tiber, we find a small chapel on the left erected in memory of the Battle of Anghiari, fought between the Milanese troups of Piccinino and the Florentines in 1440. For us, this is not so relevant in connection with the famous fresco by Leonardo in Palazzo Vecchio, Florence, which is now lost, but with the *Battle of Heraclius against Chosroes*, part of the cycle of Aretine frescoes, in which Piero could well have included passages from his visual memory of a battle fought not far from the walls of his city.

*Anton Maria Lancisi, Map of the Upper Valley of Tiber, beginning of XVIIth century, San Sepolcro, Comunità Montana.*

96

*"At the end of my life I wish to return along the road that descends into Sansepolcro, to walk down it slowly into the valley between fragile vines and tall cypresses, to find, in a house with thick walls and cool rooms, a bare bedroom and window to watch the evening descend over the valley".*

Albert Camus

*The 'Borgo' and the Upper Valley of the Tiber*

Situated at the foot of the last tract of the central Tuscan Apennines, San Sepolcro dominates the upper valley of the Tiber as it opens into a vast, yet contained, mountainous and hilly amphitheatre, bordered to the north-east by the harsh aspect of the Alpe della Luna and the Massa Trabaria, to the south by the hills of Città di Castello, and to the west by the Aretine mountains and the Alps of Catenaia. An amphitheatre, which, from time to time, changes in the picturesque quality of the valley basin with the varied and changing tones of the crops, crossed in sinuous curves by the young river Tiber — more imposing towards the Apennine arch, softer and more soffused towards the hills.

The softness of this last view suddenly changes, however, with the bristling of a rocky outline, in which the important moments and protagonists of the history of the valley seem to be grouped: the wood supplies for the Roman Trabaria, the clear outline of the Franciscan monastery of Verna, the ram of Montauto with the castle of the same name, the walled cities of Anghiari and Citerna, the wary Monte S. Maria.

"A little town surrounded by walls, set in a broad flat valley between hills", was Aldous Huxley's description of San Sepolcro in 1923. "Quietly sitting in the plane, this quite flat and comfortable city, with its lugubrious name – Borgo San Sepolcro – extends in a shell, meeting the furrows of the fields a short distance from the still green Tiber, more torrent than river."

wrote André Suarès a few years later. Once again, the truest and yet most succinct topographical description was provided in 1951 by Kenneth Clark: "Borgo San Sepolcro presents today very much the same aspect as it did in Piero's time, and everyone who has visited it has felt its affinity with his work. It lies in a flat, fertile valley framed by the upper waters of the Tiber.

On one side, close beside it are steep hills, and the mountain road which leads to Urbino; on the other, the road runs straight as a die across the valley to Anghiari and to the hills which separate the Tiber from the Arno.....And it combines, as ancient centres of a settled way of life so often do, intimacy with grandeur.

It is compact, solid, proportionate, and at its centre, made the more luminous by contrast with the narrow streets, is a white, open piazza, with a cathedral and civic offices, their arcades and pilasters rising from the slightly irregular surface of the ground as unselfconsciously as the buttresses of a barn".

The route directrices mentioned by Clark – to Florence and Urbino – refer to renaissance itineraries through Dukedoms and Principalities, crossed by Piero and described during the sixteenth and seventeenth centuries by Montaigne, Enrico II of Bourbon, Cosimo II dei Medici and many others. It is perhaps opportune to remember that San Sepolcro takes its name from a much older travelling vocation. During the Middle Ages, it was a resting place for pilgrims on their way to Rome using the route still known today as the "Romea" (Superstrada E7). In the seventeenth century – a century in which the city became a station for pilgrimages to the Franciscan sanctuaries and to Loreto – a pilgrim's chronicle notes with humour, playing with a name dear to the *homo viator* of another age: "Although Sepolcro, (Sepolto, meaning buried) the city had some splendours and a few treasures". The paintings by Piero are generally counted as "splendours" in the local eulogistic tradition. On the other hand, there were many signs of a marked and sophisticated indigenous culture which included the school of the

Agostinians; master painters with good names like Giovanni di San Sepolcro, active in Palazzo Venezia, in Rome; intarsio craftsmen with the skill of the other Giovanni, the monk responsible for the intarsio in the choirstalls of the Cathedral of Zara; local artists trained in Siena, like the already mentioned Matteo di Giovanni; quite apart from artists' work contemporary with Piero, like the extraordinary *Double-sided polyptych with the stories of St. Francis* by Sassetta, in the church bearing the same name, which today is dispersed amongst various collections and museums. From the central section of this polyptych – now at the Berenson Foundation, villa I Tatti, Florence – with "the frontal image of St. Francis, in which the expression of the divine is fixed with the static geometry of form", as Salmi writes, Piero seems to have taken a determining model for the stately frontal stance of his *Madonna della Misericordia*.

From the seventeenth to the nineteenth centuries, however, the upper valley of the Tiber and San Sepolcro remain almost

*Plan of Borgo San Sepolcro, 1900.*

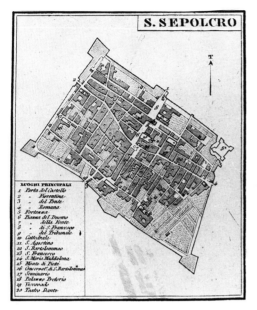

completely untouched by the passage of foreign travellers through Italy. The didactic itinerary, which during the course of the two centuries developed into a real fashion, bringing young aristocrats and wealthy bourgeoisie from all over Europe, remained stereotyped and without variation in its route. For example, the road to Siena and that less well-trodden to Arezzo were included in the journey from Florence to Rome; but in both cases the upper valley of the Tiber was neglected by foreigners and lay, forgotten in a long sleep.

As we have already seen, the road leading from Arezzo towards San Sepolcro and the Valtiberina was only "discovered", from the point of view of civilized tourism, with the unification of Italy. And it was only at the end of the century that San Sepolcro found itself on the horizons of the cultured European and American tourist's itinerary but in a rather timid and sporadic fashion. Slowly, as awareness of Piero's work increased, it became the object of rare, yet enthusiastic, pilgrimages.

*The first visitors*
This is how San Sepolcro appeared to one of the first admirers of Piero at the turn of

the century: Eugène Müntz, who arrived in the train from Arezzo, not without a little nostalgia – every era has its regrets – for the transport and methods of travelling of the past: "I would have liked to have been the last tourist to travel the twenty three miles which separate Arezzo from Borgo San Sepolcro in a carriage; in the last ten years, the railroad permits one to cover the distance in little more than two hours. Never mind: this long mountain road which passes through the picturesque city of Anghiari lacks neither surprises nor beauty. Borgo San Sepolcro is a city of extraordinary regularity, notwithstanding the slightly hilly nature of the surrounding region.

Even so, it is very picturesque and attractive. Here one sees the lively, wide 'Via Maestra',illuminated by oil lamps, its Renaissance palazzi – solid, tranquil, wide buildings – alternate with comfortable bourgeois houses in which bricks (demonstrating Umbria's vicinity) mingle with stone; there, empty roads disappear into the distance ...in the intervals, delightful corners: some decorated with hanging gardens, cultivated with care and full of laurel; others hiding overgrown gardens, invaded by weeds, by wild flowers, by giant rose-bushes. At times, at the end of a street, the view of a mountain enlivens the prospect. The picture is filled by people coming and going in no great hurry; in the doorways, women intent on spinning. The Piazza del Municipio has important buildings all around it: the cathedral, the Town Hall, with the District Magistrate's Court and the Royal Security Delegation, constructed in antique style, in stone; these are decorated with ancient coats-of-arms in polychrome terracotta. Leaving to one side a fine collection of interesting, but second class works, the tourist should view the *Resurrection,* painted in fresco by the most famous native artist of Borgo San Sepolcro, Piero della Francesca, in a room in the Town Hall. With this example of great mastery, of regal impassiveness, Piero prepared the way for the great Andrea Mantegna, who honoured him with an imitation of his work in the museum of Tours."

*Plan of Borgo San Sepolcro, 1856, San Sepolcro, Private Collection.*

In the gradual discovery of Piero and his city by people like Müntz, who were capable of spreading his name throughout Europe, these words have great innovative value, even if they are not exempt from a slight uncertainty. On one hand Müntz understands the greatness of Piero in the regality of his figures, on the other, he still seems to evaluate their message in terms of other painters. It cannot be ignored, however, that his method of interpreting the urban setting of San Sepolcro, particularly the emphasis placed on topographical tranquility and regularity, is marked by a certain atmospheric quality of Piero della Francesca.

With the turn of the century, more sophisticated civilizations had already learnt to appreciate, as J.A.Symonds wrote in 1875, the most sublime, most poetic and most awful interpretation ever realized of the Resurrection.

The *Resurrection* is already included in the most widely used guide books well before the affrescoes in Arezzo are mentioned; for example, the *Cities of Central Italy*

*(1876)* by A.J. Cuthbert Hare: "It is early morning in a wintry landscape, a valley in a wild Umbrian country, with great trees breaking the sky. In the centre is the tomb from which the Saviour is rising grandly and triumphantly, with one foot on the ledge, a banner with a red cross in his right hand, and his eyes looking forward with rapt integrity, the whole figure thrown out by the blackness of the hills behind, upon which the light has not yet risen. Below lie, or rather sit, the four guards, greatly foreshortened, in the most intense sleep."

*The Lost Heritage*

The works of Piero, which still remain in San Sepolcro, are now reunited in the Civic Museum, in the room dominated by the fresco of the *Resurrection*. Before proceeding with their description, it is opportune to recall some of the works which the city has lost over the centuries, because it is *those* works which bear the signs of Piero's very particular and continuous relationship with the city of his birth.

The panel with the *Baptism of Christ*,

*Panorama of San Sepolcro, XXth century lithograph.*

usually considered to be a youthful work of the artist, was sold by the Chapter of the Cathedral of San Sepolcro in 1859. This was almost contemporary with the private sale abroad of the last work of Piero, the *Nativity*. The history of this double sale was reconstructed a few years later by the buyer, J.C. Robinson, in an article in the "Times", of which we include the following eloquent passages: "In 1859 I was commissioned by Her Majesty's Government to make researches and acquisitions of works of art in Italy.

That country was in a state of war and revolution, and the unsettlements of things in general afforded unusual facilities for my purpose ..... At Borgo San Sepolcro, a mountain town on the skirts of the central Apennines, I found that, in spite of troubled times and universal penury, the ecclesiastical authorities of the place were bent on 'restoring' (in reality, desecrating with cheap bedizenment) the interior of the ancient cathedral....

The church was gutted and its ancient furniture and pictures, and the latter, among which were two invaluable works of great historic note, were stored away in adjoining offices. One of these was the Baptism of Christ by Piero della Francesca, now in the National Gallery.....While at Borgo, I was informed that two young gentlemen, the Signori Marini-Franceschi, descendants of Piero della Francesca, had recently inherited an undoubted work of the master (the Nativity, now in the National Gallery), and that they sent it to Florence for sale."

Quite apart from the intrinsic value of these two works, it is essential to underline the iconic connection, which links them to the upper valley of the Tiber and to San Sepolcro. We should consider the valley depicted in the *Baptism*; a true garden of delights watered by the young Tiber with the city in the background, the name of which already alludes to the destiny of Christ in the act of being baptized. We must also remember the urban perspective on the right side of the *Nativity*, in which the viewer finds the exact topographical representation of the centre of San Se-

*J. Pennell, View of Borgo San Sepolcro, 1899,*
*Florence Uffizi.*

*J. Pennell, La torre di Berta, 1899, Florence,*
*Uffizi.*

*A. Terreni, View with the Palazzo delle Laudi*
*and the Cathedral.*

*View of the Cathedral and the Palazzo delle*
*Laudi, lithograph.*

*Palazzo delle Laudi, lithograph.*

*Piazza Garibaldi, lithograph.*

102

polcro, metaphorically Bethlehem and simultaneously the city of birth and death.
In the century before this, San Sepolcro had lost the splendid, and for us, mysterious, altar panel of Sant'Agostino – the surviving small panels are to be found in various museums. We only know that it was on sale, already in fragments, in Milan at the end of the eighteenth century.
Finally, in 1903, the Collacchioni family sold the *Hercules* from palazzo Graziani to the collection of Isabella Stewart Gardner through a Florentine antique dealer. Palazzo Graziani was Piero's house, in which he had represented the *Hercules* with his attributes of strength, the club, and of reflection, his hand on his hip, as an emblem of heroic virtue, in deep contrast to the obsessive fury with which this figure was normally associated.
Let us now analyse more closely the works of Piero in the Civic Museum of San Se-

polcro, starting with the most representative and emblematic figure of all, the risen Christ.

*The Resurrection*
Adopting the language of local heraldry, the *Resurrection* has become the emblem of the city for the figurative way in which it narrates a story which took place centuries before its appellative. It should be mentioned that the name is derived from the relics of San Sepolcro bought from the Holy Land by two pilgrims – Arcano and Egidio – who were ordered to conclude their journey in the upper valley of the Tiber and to found a city. The emblematic connection between San Sepolcro and the *Resurrection*, two moments in the same story, has been observed not only by writers and art historians but also by the most humble of tourist guides. It is not, therefore, surprising to find references to the

risen Christ in terms of an actual *genus loci* – or guardian spirit of the place – we can refer to the "sylvan and almost bovine Christ" of Longhi, the "wild grandiosity of the resurrected Christ" of Camus, of even the "country God ...worshipped from the moment man understood that the seed did not die in the winter earth", of Clark. Even if one purifies him of all aesthetic overtones, the Christ of the *Resurrection* does not completely give up his totemic function for the upper valley of the Tiber, so that for one moment in the eye of the beholder, that valley and that city become a metaphor for the whole world. This ritualistic and totemic role – as well as the open geometric eloquence with which divine charisma is expressed – is the reason for the unconditioned admiration and the fullness of the epithets which accompany the critical history of the painting from the admiration of Vasari to Aldous Huxley's "

best painting in the world".

The symbology itself of the fresco aids the exaltation of this mythical dimension, of this gradiose rite of fertility, both pagan and christian at the same time; from the pink mantle referring to the new dawn of Christ's resurrection, to the two lines of trees, bare on the left of the fresco, and green on the right, indicating the rebirth of nature and the advent of a new era for mankind.

Emphasis has often been laid on the geometric structure of the affresco: the head of Christ at the top of an equilateral triangle, the intersection of the diagonals of a square painted in the umbilicus of the rising figure, the elevation of Christ on a higher plane than that upon which the soldiers rest, providing the beholder with a double viewpoint. This last fact seems fundamental in rendering the figure of Christ even more impressive, as it uses a more

*Via Niccolò Aggiunti, lithograph.*

*Palazzo Ducci Del Rosso, lithograph.*

*Piero della Francesca gardens and apse
of S. Francesco, lithograph.*

*Arch of S. Chiara, lithograph.*

*Piazza di S. Chiara, lithograph.*

*Church of S. Francesco, lithograph.*

*Monument to Piero della Francesca, lithograph.*

elevated viewpoint than that placed on the sarcophagus, by which the sleeping soldiers are seen from below, "opened up like four segments of fruit", to use Longhi's expression.

In 1924 the English writer, Aldous Huxley, suggested another implication of the fresco by Piero della Francesca neglected by the art critics; the fact that the figure of the resurrected is "more like a Plutarchian hero than the Christ of conventional religion", and therefore the whole painting is,"the resurrection of the classical ideal, incredibly much grander and more beautiful than the classical reality, from the tomb where it had lain so many hundred years". This interpretation certanly does not con-

tradict the others, and can also be connected to the political destination of the fresco, realized for the public room of the Palazzo dei Conservatori of San Sepolcro. Indeed, all Piero's works can be seen as the most mature, conscious, austere synthesis of humanist-christian values. A synthesis which concedes nothing, on one hand, to the programmatic staging of antique remains, nor on the other to the caressing, ornamental narration of a religious message. The powerful evocative sensation with which we are invariably affected when observing the *Resurrection* by Piero is due, in the last analysis, to this archaic mixture of strength and wisdom.

We have mentioned the possible interpre-

*Piero della Francesca, Resurrection, detail with a soldier, Borgo San Sepolcro, Civic Museum.*

*Piero della Francesca, Resurrection, detail with a soldier, considered by local tradition to be a self-portrait, Borgo San Sepolcro, Civic Museum.*

tations which art critics has provided of this fresco, the sacred restoration of Christ who emerges from the altar-like tomb, not forgetful of the ancestral fears of a nature which must renew itself.

Piero was familiar with one iconographic example of the Risen Christ to be found in the present cathedral of San Sepolcro; the *Polyptych of the Resurrection* by a Sienese artist (Niccolo di Segna?). But in order to prove once again the force with which Piero della Francesca's work could impose itself on the visitor, the following is documentary evidence, written by travellers who observed the work of art with so-called "profane" eyes, before the diffusion of the words of Berenson or of Longhi. The first of our travellers is a writer who dedicated many volumes to Italy, its regions and its roads. The words of Maurel on the *Resurrection* of Piero, entitled *Christ the Avenger*, were published in 1912: "The whole work is contained within an equilateral triangle; its apex formed by the head of Christ, and its base by the marble sarcophagus, the straight line of which occupies the bottom of the fresco. Thus delineated, the work acquires an incomparable serenity. A cold mathematics which elevates the spirit with the force of its solid construction.

This purity of line, harvested in the immediacy of the spirit, assumes the nature of an indisputable theorem, and as such, imposes itself. Piero's talent was able to move emotionally. And this is the task of the artist strictly subjected to nature. Above all, outside the triangle, that which evokes the dream, the poetry: the background divided into two, on one side a desolate landscape, on the other luxuriant; admirable the subtle contrast between the two. On the right, soft hills, light, feathery trees; on the left, arid mountains and great, bare trees. Nature is resuscitated alongside its own death to announce the miracle .....In San Sepolcro one can contemplate one of the most complete works of art in existence, because it includes everything: a new idea based on scientific rules and realized with an art more confident of itself."

Little more than ten years after Maurel,

another French traveller and lover of Italy, Suarès, dedicated memorable words to "Piero the Great". Here is a significant extract which deals with some rather different aspects than those considered by Maurel: "Piero is never sentimental. He never looks for originality: he naturally possesses it because he does not think like others. He is powerful: this is his highest virtue. He knows exactly how to achieve grace, when he so wishes, just like any other expression, except voluptuousness. But his real enchantment is that of full strength, young but not too young: strength and nothing else. He, who in my opinion is the most modern of Italian painters, is the only one who makes me think of Greek painting. Am I fantasizing? Perhaps. But I that is what I think. His Christ is a Zeus. Nevertheless, before leaving the tomb, Christ had to die.

He will depart from the double night – death and the dream of mankind – only after he has suffered the death of mankind."

We have mentioned above a work by Aldous Huxley. As is often the case with travel writers, his text could be said to have "saved" the painting. In actual fact, the incisive and peremptory title – "the most beautiful painting in the world" – contributed in 1944, with the progress of the war front, in saving Piero's *Resurrection* from the canonfire, as Anthony Clarke, artillery officer with the task of bombing San Sepolcro, recalls: "At the back of my mind a small question kept nagging. Why did I know that name of Sansepolcro? Somewhere I had heard the name and it must have been in connection with something important for me to remember it. But when and where I could not remember."

Then it dawned on him: "I must have been about eighteen when I read that essay of Aldous Huxley's. I recalled clearly his description of the tiring journey from Arezzo and how it was worth it for at the end lay Francesca's *Resurrection*, "the greatest painting in the world!" ...I estimated the number of shells I had fired and was sure that if I had not destroyed the greatest painting I had done considerable damage. So I fired no more ......The next day we

*Piero della Francesca, St. Ludovico,*
*Borgo San Sepolcro, Civic Museum.*

*Piero della Francesca, St. Julian,*
*Borgo San Sepolcro, Civic Museum.*

entered Sansepolcro unmolested. I asked immediately for the picture. The building was untouched. I hurried inside and there it was, secure and magnificent. The townsfolk had started to sandbag it, but the sandbags were only about waist-high. I looked up at the roof: one shell, I knew, would have been sufficient to undo the admiration of centuries. And that is that. Sometimes I wonder how I would be feeling now if I had happened to destroy the *Resurrection*. At one time I thought of writing to Aldous Huxley. The incident might, I suppose, be a fine illustration of the power of literature, and that the pen is mightier than the sword!"

*The Madonna della Misericordia*
This is believed to be a youthful work of Piero, even though it was painted over a long period of time. The polyptych was, in fact, commissioned by the local fraternity of the Misericordia in 1445 for the altar of their church. It seems only to have been completed in 1460. The actual composition of the sections and panels is hypothetical, as the original framework has been lost, seriously affecting the whole. In the centre of the polyptych the Madonna of the Misericordia gathers the faithful together under her cloak – a quite popular and frequent iconographic image in the Aretine region. We need only refer to the *Madonne della Misericordia* by Parri Spinelli and by Lorentino d'Arezzo, which we have already briefly mentioned. The traditional taste, probably of the patron, is also reflected in the gold ground.
Notwithstanding this, Piero's modernity contrasts profoundly with this taste. Recalling the frescoes of S. Francesco in Arezzo, the open cone of the mantle becomes once again the geometric icon of the composition culminating in the cylindrical neck and the spherical head of the Madonna. One could provide an explanation for the regality of Piero's figures in this attempt to lead the physical indivualities of the body into a sort of geometrical archetype; the intuition of a universal law.
The entire *Polyptych of the Misericordia* is a real palimpsest; the different stages and styles of Piero della Francesca's art and his

assistants, who played an important part, particularly in the surrounding figures, are all present in this work. It is not by chance that in a skilful antiphrasis to the pure geometry used for the figure of the Madonna, the faithful gathered beneath her mantle reveal a varied and acute portraiture, recalling the physiognomic taste of Domenico Veneziano and in contrast to those dramatic positions used in the Crucifixion of the cymatium, influenced by Masaccio, there is a new and diverse sensitivity of Flemish descent, found in the luministic and tactile values of the materials and flesh tones of the figures, modelled in light.
Clark dedicates some of his most intense passages to this work. He points out the general canons of Piero's art and with them, the reasons for his long eclipse from the panorama of Western art: "Piero had the power of creating forms which immediately satisfy us by their completeness; forms which reconcile the mathematical laws of proportion with the stress and tension of growth, forms which combine the resilience of a tree trunk with the precision of a pre-dynastic jar. Such concentration on pure form places a certain restraint on those inflections which communicate sentiment; and the Virgin has that air of remoteness which early admirers of Piero, brought up on the languorous glances of the Pre-Raphaelites or the unabashed rhetoric of Raphael, found so cold and aloof. For this reason she has been compared to those images embodying the spiritual state of non-attachment to which the Far Eastern religions aspire. But set her beside the smiling Buddha heads of Indo-China or China itself, and how strongly she asserts her Mediterranean humanity! Behind her serenity there is even something stubbornly sensual, which means, perhaps, no more than that she is a young peasant, part of the creative process which is her occupation and which has taught her the need for mercy and protection".

*St. Julian*
The other great example of Piero's work in the Civic Museum of San Sepolcro is the

*Luca Signorelli, Crucifixion,*
*Borgo San Sepolcro, Civic Museum.*

*Piero della Francesca, Hercules, Boston,*
*Isabella Stewart Gardner Museum.*

*Polyptych with the Risen Christ, Sienese School, Borgo San Sepolcro, Cathedral.*

fresco representing (in Salmi's opinion) *St Julian* – discovered by chance during the cleaning of rooms already in the possession of the church of S. Chiara (the ancient church of St. Augustine) in 1954 and detached in 1957. This was one of the most important discoveries of renaissance art.

Although there has been a tendency to perceive certain psychological nuances in this work, such as anger, unusual in the imperturbable art of Piero, there are the typical characteristics of a geometric stylization. These are accented in the spherical volume of the face onto which the fleshy nose and mouth are flattened, whereas the triangular cut of the eyes frames round, wide pupils.

As in the finest examples of his work, this detracts nothing from the softness of the flesh and the delicacy of the rhythms of Piero's preferred colours, balanced between green and velvet carmine.

*St. Ludovico*

The *St. Ludovico* is attributed to an assistant of Piero, perhaps Lorentino, work of whom we have already seen in Arezzo.

It is a fresco detached from a room in the Palazzo Pretoria where it had been commissioned by Lodovico Acciaioli, Governor of the Borgo in 1460.

The half figure, almost totally frontal, has the usual regality of Piero della Francesca's figures, even if the colour of the fresco is somewhat subdued.

*St. Sebastian*

This detached fresco from the church of the nearby hamlet of Gricignano is related to Piero's influence even if some of his traditional stylistic attributes appear very weak.

*Other Works in the Civic Museum*

There are other works of art in the Civic

Museum, suggestive in their own right, strictly linked to the presence or direct influence of Piero in his home town.

This visit could begin with the two lateral parts of a triptych, representing *St. Peter* and *St. Paul* within a very elaborate structure with small panels of saints on pilasters and a predella.

The triptych, a work by Matteo di Giovanni (circa 1430 – 1495), a painter from San Sepolcro trained in Siena, had always been planned to include the *Baptism* by Piero della Francesca and the latter was in fact inserted into the framework in about 1480. This was originally situated in the priory of S. Giovanni Battista, or on the altar of that name in the cathedral, but at the beginning of the nineteenth century the triptych was in the cathedral and then temporarily placed in the sacristy, as mentioned by Robinson, who acquired the *Baptism* in 1859. Today, it is not easy to imagine how the rocky, airy landscape of the central part of the *Baptism* could have been compatible with the framework and late-Gothic lateral panels by Matteo di Giovanni. In any case, the scenes of the predella are particularly beautiful; they recount the story of St. John the Baptist, protagonist together with the baptized Christ of Piero's panel, and patron saint of the church, up to Salome's fatal dance.

Another example of Piero's influence in his home town are the *tarsie* in polychrome wood which decorate the backs of the fifteenth century *choir* from the church of St. Francis. This consists of sixteen stalls, in four groups of four each. The structure of the choir is still Gothic, whereas the tarsia, with landscapes and townscapes alternating with groups of objects, have a totally new treatment. The views of the city, in particular, are marked by a perspective essentiality which caused Salmi to name Piero as their creator. The checquered pavement of one of the piazze with a loggia "seems to be a descendant of that in the "Flagellation" in Urbino".

One compact and essential view of a city could be based on San Sepolcro as it appeared in the fifteenth century before the Medicean fortifications begun by Giuliano da Sangallo.

In the adjacent room to that containing the work of Piero, there is an interesting painting which some maintain to have a hint of Piero della Francesca. This is the *Assumption of the Virgin with Apostles and Saints*, dated to the beginning of the sixteenth century. The scene is divided into two superimposed parts: above, the Madonna within a mandorla surrounded by angels, below, a landscape of Peruginesque sensitivity, framed by four saints. The altar-panel comes from St. Augustine, then the Church of S. Chiara, where, in the second half of the sixteenth century, it substituted the lost polyptych of Piero della Francesca.

The hypothesis that the central panel is that of the polyptych by Piero della Francesca, partially ideated by Piero himself and painted in the following century, is no longer credible. The attribution is uncertain.

Following this, there is the two-sided *Processional banner* by Luca Signorelli (1445 circa-1523), the most famous pupil of Piero. This work was realized in about 1505, after the frescoes for the Chapel of St. Brizio in the Cathedral of Orvieto, and mark Signorelli's full, autonomous maturity.

The processional standard, original both in its intrinsic pictorial value and for its traditional function, was realized by Signorelli for the Compagnia di S. Antonio Abate of San Sepolcro.

On one side, St. Antonio Abate and St. Egidio with the habitual insistence of Signorelli for tones of brown, and the metallic polish of the limbs; on the other side, the Crucifixion, characterized by a lively yet sinuous design which links together the figures at the base of the Cross.

The landscape with its disappearing perspective of slanting crosses and a square construction in a frame of imaginary rocks is clear and deep.

In the upper valley of the Tiber we will discover several works by Signorelli which function as authentic tributes to the maestro of the Borgo.

Let us conclude this brief visit within the Civic Museum in search of memories of Piero della Francesca with a *Votive panel*, which invokes the liberation of the plague.

*Monatery of Montecasale, lithograph.*

*View of Urbino, end of XIXth century.*

It comes from the Misericordia di S. Rocco and represents some hooded monks with a stretcher. The inscription invokes the protection of the Madonna for a pilgrimage about to depart for Loreto. Behind the stretcher, there is a panoramic view of San Sepolcro, "A little town, surrounded by walls, set in a broad flat valley between hills", Huxley was to write centuries later. The exact view of this *Votive panel* remains the best sixteenth century view of the Borgo, of its valley, of the Tiber and, in the distant hills, of Citerna and Anghiari.

*The Cathedral*
The whole city is so rich in memories of Piero della Francesca – the regular plan of its streets, the proportion of its palazzi, the unmistakeable outline of the bell-towers with their pyramidal spires, so often "quoted" by Piero – that this journey in search of the town's great artist could not be complete without a visit to the city itself.
As far as direct connections to Piero are concerned, we should study two important historic monuments.
The first is the cathedral which, in the upper valley of the Tiber, is perhaps the most complex building in its foundation of two different architectural styles, Romanesque and Gothic; indeed Salmi defines it as a "Romanesque structure with Gothic proportions".
From the beginning of this millenium, when the church was founded, up until 1520, it was a Camaldolite abbey. This would explain the influence of the Camaldolite abbots on the iconographic choices of Piero to which we have already referred and in particular, to the *Baptism*, housed here up until 1859, in which the three angels assisting the ceremony symbolize the union of the churches.
The building underwent various modifications and restructuring, amongst these, the refacing of the bell-tower in 1352 following an earthquake. It was terminated, above the bell-cell, with an attic of brick and a high pyramidal spire with a square base, inspired by an Umbrian tradition, which first appeared in San Sepolcro with the church and bell-tower of S. Francesco. As far as the numerous, and important,

works conserved in the Cathedral are concerned, we have already mentioned the polytypch, sometimes attributed to Niccolò di Segna with its central panel figuring the *Resurrection.*
For the other works, we refer the reader to more specialized publications, with the addition, however, of the extraordinary documentary evidence of pilgrims bound for Loreto half way through the seventeenth century. Stopping in the cathedral, they refer briefly to paintings which they had observed in this "small city, but populated by many significant paintings: here you can see in the Cathedral two saints at the middle door, work of Pier della Francesca, a chapel of the abbot, an altar-panel on the high altar of S. Agostino, in S. Gilio a panel by Pietro Perugino, in the Compagnia di S. Croce a panel by Rosso, in S. Francesco a painting of S. Quintino by Pontormo".
These words written by an unknown Sienese pilgrim are sufficient information on which to base an evocative city tour, and above all, they indicate the presence of two saints "at the middle door", of which every trace has now been lost.

*The house of Piero*
The other essential reference point in the city is the house of Piero della Francesca in via Aggiunte, in front of the bell-tower of S. Francesco and the public gardens. This now consists of a refined, if probably altered, example of fifteenth century architecture.
The presence of design details by Michelozzo in the portal, the windows and the corbels inside is, according to Salmi, evidence of the influence of the palazzo ducale of Urbino; and therefore, the possibility that Piero designed the house cannot be excluded. Regarding this palazzo, there is the interesting testimony of an American traveller, Egerton R. Williams, who visited it in 1903, a few days before the *Hercules* was sold.
Here are a few passages from his text: "After this I spent some time in strolling about the town …till I brought up against a little park on the first rise of the mountain side, decorated with an excellent marble statue of Piero della Francesca.

*Romayne Robert, The Bell-Tower of S.*
*Francesco, travel note-book, circa 1896.*

Near the park, in the private palace of the Collachioni, is his reputed *chef d'oeuvre,* – the Infant Hercules. A worthy citizen conducted me to the palace – which had an exterior as ugly and dull as any other – and a pompous *portiere* admitted me, in the absence of the family.

The interior was as rich and elaborate as the outside was plain, which is typical of Italian houses generally. There was a handsome lower hall, with suites of living-rooms, parlors, and billiard room opening off to right and left; and at the end was a curving stone stairway that led to a smaller hall on the first floor, adorned with arms and armor.

From this opened a spacious salon of seventeenth century style, with frescoed ceiling and table of precious marble, and here upon the end wall was Piero's painting of the Infant Hercules, — a sturdy, bare-limbed child, aglow with vigorous strength, a true precursor of Luca Signorelli's ath-letes in his Last Judgement at Orvieto."

After this description of an interior of a noble palazzo, we will leave Borgo San Sepolcro with a page dedicated to its celebrated cuisine.

On this subject, let us quote the art historian, P.G. Konody, with his usual liveliness and subtle malice, in his book on travels in Italy, completed in 1909. Konody arrived in San Sepolcro from Urbino in one of the first automobile journeys, dripping with rain: "My first and only fixed impression of *Sansepolcro* is a spacious, busy kitchen, with a grateful wood-fire, with steaming kettle and dishes, and two buxom, solicitous women — one of them of strikingly handsome features — bustling about me, pulling off an overcoat and coat, the sleeves of which were clinging to my soaking wet shirt-sleeves, hanging up the garments to dry, and placing a chair for me bythe glowing embers. It was not a little tantalising to see the contents of a huge pot of particularly appetising aroma diminish and vanish into nothing, as dish after dish was filled with the savoury stew and carried into the dining-room, but there was no help. I had to get dry before I could join the others at their meal; and when I did join them, it was too late for that tempting *plat-du-jour*, thanks to the approval with which it had met from a large and merry wedding or birthday party of country-folk who had chosen this unpropitious day to come "to town". Too late for everything but an improvised cutlet and some cheese!"

*Other City Itineraries*
As we have been told by various foreign travellers from the last and the beginning of this centuries, San Sepolcro and its valley offers many other interesting itineraries. It seems unnecessary to discuss other routes within the town; San Sepolcro, within the limited quadrangle of the Medicean walls and the only slightly varied checquered pattern of its streets, is to be enjoyed at a pedestrian pace.
Let us follow for a short way the American tourist who visited the town in 1903: "All of Sansepolcro is primitive — from the mediaeval brick battlements and moat to the narrow roughly paved street with their crumbling stuccoed houses. It has the air of the Middle Ages, unswept by the breath of modern improvements; and it has the aspect of poverty, in spite of the rich valley that lies around. The streets are fairly rectangular, lying as they do upon the plain, and but few buildings of distinction rise from the mass of brown roofs that extend to the slope of the mountain.
From the northern gate, where I entered, the main street extends for nearly a mile to the southern gate. I passed along it to the Piazza in the centre, stopping to observe en route an extraordinary medieval frieze over one of the shops (now in the Sala delle pietre of the Civic Museum) .....The Piazza groups round an isolated campanile (the Torre di Berta, blown up by the Germans in 1945), the centre and the loftiest building of the town. It was constructed of cut stone centuries ago, by the citizens at the height of their pride, as an ornament and

bell-tower for the city. Its ornamental qualities are now impaired by the crumbling away of the stones and mortar from the corners aloft, leaving jagged lines against the sky, but the bells still ring out on every possible occasion.
On the south side of the Piazza rises a rather handsome old palace with well-proportioned window-frames of rusticated stone set in the plaster facade; it is the best looking building in Sansepolcro. On the north extends a line of shops, in the ground floors of edifices that once were noble dwellings, as is indicated by the remnants of medieval towers that they raise here and there. To the east is a narrower extension of the Piazza, more picturesque than the wide space, with the little Municipio on the left, approached by a flight of steps, and the plain cathedral on the right. Beyond the cathedral rolls the renaissance arcade of the Palazzo dei Marini, now used as the law courts. A wall here ends the Piazza, having an archway through which I caught a glimpse of a white house in the street beyond, with a pretty loggia on the first floor."
The only work of art, contemporary with Piero, reamining outside this itinerary, is the beautiful scalloped altar-piece with the *Assumption of the Virgin* in the church of S. Maria dei Servi; we leave the rest to a more specific guide dealing with an integral excursion of the city.
Amongst the itineraries outside the city, it is worth remembering a series of routes of noticeable artistic, cultural and naturalistic interest: the "naturalist's" choice, which follows the upper Tiber, the "mountaineer's" route through the Alpe della Luna, and the "mystic" itinerary that leads to the Franciscan convents. These are routes famous throughout Europe and entire publications have been dèdicated to them, from the already mentioned volume by the pre-raphaelite, Davies, on the Tiber to that of Beryl de Selincourt, and many others after her, on the dwelling places of the first Franciscans.

*The Valley of Pliny*
Even in the schematic and summarized tourist's view, the guardianship of Piero

*Plaque with an episode in the life of St. Francis, Montecasale.*

della Francesca of his native ground, that guardianship which led him to reiterate with lucid topography the outline of his city and the rotundity of his mountains, reveals the secret code of an ancestral relationship, which is translated for us into an extraordinary lesson in analysis and interpretation of landscape.

The city and valley appeared to Piero, in actual fact, not as a setting for his own family story, but as an example of a serene, ideal, classic landscape suggested by the epistles of Pliny the Younger with the description of his villa *in Tuscis*, recalled by ancient travellers. Pliny's description, in his letter to Domizio Apollinare (V,6 ), which is so evocative of the essential beauty of the place in terms of a happy microcosm, harmonious in every one of its ingredients — "imagine a great amphitheatre, one that only nature is capable of creating" — describes itself the manner in which artists and topographists recreated the valtiberian context: "You would experience intense delight if you were to view this region from the hills above: it would seem, in fact, that you did not look upon the land itself, but on a painting executed with incredible skill; of so much variety and of such a happy disposition that the viewer is delighted, whichever way he looks."

The upper valley of the Tiber, in which Piero sets many ritual scenes, is an extraordinary example of a synthesis between christian and humanist iconography.

The humanist model is one of ideal environmental beauty, of a natural amphitheatre elevated by metaphor to the status of a universe, complete in itself, populated by signs which allude to other stories and other legends.

In iconographic symbology, the upper Tiber is confused with the Jordan and establishes a typically and premonitory humanist link between pagan and christian history in the weave of diverse, yet complimentary, destinies.

The city, finally, which appears in the background of the paintings — of the *Baptism*, the *St. Jerome*, the *Nativity* — is, even in its name, a simulacrum of the tomb of Christ and his inheritance to mankind; it

is the city born to guard his memory and his name.

Considering this, one could quote the words of an ancient chronicler: "our land of Borgo San Sepolcro was called the New Jerusalem", a Jerusalem chosen by happy chance in the lap of Pliny's valley.

*Towards Urbino*

It is not the task of this guide to venture beyond the Borgo of Piero, although, as I have already mentioned, the entire artistic parabola of Piero della Francesca can be reconstructed in the brief tract on each side of the Appennines, between the valleys of the Arno and the Tiber, along which we have travelled, and that of the high Metauro.

It is known that for a long time Piero was guest of the Dukes of Urbino; indeed two of his greatest pictorial masterpieces are today conserved in the Ducal Palace; the *Flagellation* and the *Madonna di Senigallia*.

It is also known that Piero worked in Rimini for the Malatesta and that the superb fresco of *Sigismondo Pandolfo Malatesta* is conserved in the Tempio Malatestiano.

More than one empassioned traveller can be our guide, on another occasion, over the other side of Appennines and in the valleys of the Metauro and the Foglia, from J.A. Symonds, Vernon Lee and Aldous Huxley to the old, and ever admirable, Montaigne.

*Towards Città di Castello*

The upper valley of the Tiber, however, holds in reserve other routes through Um-

122

brian lands, which contain further evidence of the world in which the figure of Piero stands out. Descending a few kilometres into the valley, following the main road or the Superstrada E7, one reaches a city with a distinctive outline, scattered with beautiful renaissance palaces surrounding the Ravenna-type bell-tower of the Cathedral. This is Città di Castello "which had the Tiber at its walls where delicate fish are to be found", as Piccolpasso notes. A city which for centuries remained on the very edge of didactic and pleasurable travels, and therefore also of the modern tourist. This prolonged exclusion from the main travel routes, even more extreme that that of San Sepolcro, is noted by more than one nineteenth century traveller.

For example, let us refer to the arrival of the pre-raphaelite, Davies, together with the American, Vedder, to the city in 1872: "It was high noon as we entered Città di Castello. Every blind and door was closed to the sun. As we rattled along the dazzling white pavement not a soul was visible, not even a dog. It was like a city of the dead. By the deserted loggia long green vinesprays dangled in the sun. Grass grew in the streets. In the heart of a large town we were in perfect solitude."

Only a few years ago, in 1969, Maurice Rowdon described Città di Castello with notable clarity, without concealing a taste for intellectual discovery. He noted that for those coming from the north, it is an excellent introduction to Umbria: for it is not quite the mystic Umbria to be discovered later, but has a persistance of Tuscan luminosity, a vestige perhaps of the Florentine canon.

Two important testimonies await us in the splendid city art gallery. One is the panel with tempera of the *Benediction of Christ*, which has been considered a Flemish imitation (Giusto di Gand?) of Piero della Francesca. The other represents one of the masterpieces of Signorelli's career: the great altar-panel of the *Martyrdom of S. Sebastiano*. Let us remember Signorelli once again, as Piero's pupil, because not far from Castello, descending into the valley of the Tiber, in the city of Umbertide, the ancient Fratta, we find a moving and very revealing indication of the relationship between pupil and master. This is the *Deposition from the Cross* (1515 — 1517); Signorelli included a scene in the predella with the stories of the Cross, which repeats in the form of an homage, Piero's Battle of Constantine against Maxentius in S. Francesco in Arezzo.

We also find in Città di Castello a *Madonna with Child and Saints Florido and Crescentino* by Giovanni da Piamonte, already encountered as Piero's assistant in the Aretine affrescoes.

Other hints and traces of Piero della Francesca in Umbria could easily be mentioned, but this would lead to an excessive detour from our route so we can but mention the great *Polyptych* by Piero della Francesca in the National Gallery of Umbria: occasion for another journey and other cultural adventures.

# Guides and Travelling Companions

*Michel Eyquem de Montaigne.*

*Johann Wolfang von Goethe.*

*Michel Eyquem De Montaigne (1533-1592)*
French writer and creator of the literary form of the "essay" which bears the title *Essais*. In 1580-81, he completed a long journey through Germany and Italy, inspiring his *Journal de Voyage en Italie par la Suisse et l'Allemagne* (Travel Journal in Italy, through Switzerland and Germany) published almost two centuries after his death in 1774. The journal is partly written in Italian by Montaigne himself and partly in French by his secretary.

*Fynes Moryson (1566-circa 1614)*
English writer and traveller. His travel journal, *Itinerary Containing his Ten Year's Travel*, was published posthumously in London in 1617. Some chapters concerning Italian customs, not included in this volume, were published in London in 1903 with the title, *Shakespeare's Europe*. His work is considered one of the first guides for the use of British, French and German travellers and was enormously successful during the course of the seventeenth century.

*Joseph Furttenbach (1591-1667)*
A German polygraph, he was in Italy from 1606 to 1615. On his return to Germany, he transmitted his love of Italian architecture

to his contemporaries. His *Newes Itinerarium Italiae*, written in German and published in Ulm in 1627, was considered the true "Baedecker of the seventeenth century" for its division into itineraries, and the indication of places of naturalistic and artistic beauty. He also registered those routes across the peninsular which were destined to fall into oblivion with the advent of the *Grand Tour*.

*Tobias Smollet (1721-1771)*
Scottish writer, author of novels with a picaresque flavour, such as *Roderick Random*, *Peregrine Prickle* and *Humphrey Clinker*. His acid and satyrical, if not humourless, spirit appears in his volume dedicated to the *Grand Tour* in 1764 and entitled *Travels Through France and Italy*, 1766. A consumptive, he undertook a journey to Italy in 1770 and the following year died near Livorno.

*Johann Wolfgang Von Goethe (1794-1832)*
Born in Frankfurt-on-Main, he was the son of an imperial advisor. He studied law at the University of Leipzig and passed much of his time at the Court of Weimar, where he held various posts and wrote his most famous works. His double journey to Italy, in 1786 to 1788 and in 1790, had an important influence on his development and produced *Italienishe Reise* written in the form of a brief diary and letters written to friends. The *Romischen Elegien*, compositions in classic metre, are also linked to his Italian sojourn.

124 *Samuel Rogers (1763-1855)*
English poet and man of letters, he travelled in Italy between 1814 and 1815, during the course of which he kept a diary, the *Italian Journal*, only published in 1956, from which are taken the annotations on Camucia. In 1822, his poem, *Italy*, was published with illustrations by Turner, Prout and Harding, followed by numerous editions.

*Stendhal, pseudonym for Henri Beyle (1783-1842)*
Born in Grenoble, as a young man he served as an officer in the Napoleonic forces. After the Restoration, he lived for many years in Italy, and was consul in Trieste and Civitavecchia from 1830 to 1841, but later he returned to France and died in Paris. His greatest novels are *Le Rouge et le Noir*, 1830, and *Le Chartreuse de Parme*, 1839. On Italy, he wrote *Rome, Naples et Florence and Promenades dans Rome*, which represents one of the highest travel literature.

*Sidney, Lady Morgan (1732-1821)*
Daughter of an Irish actor fallen on hard times, she maintained her family by becoming a governess and then a writer. In 1812, she married Sir Thomas Charles Morgan, and thus acquired her title. Amongst her most famous works is a book dedicated to the life and times of Salvator Rosa. In 1819-1820 she undertook a voyage to Italy and the famous work, *Italy*, was published in 1821.

*William Brockedon (1787-1852)*
English writer and artist, he was a member of the Academies for the Arts in Rome and in Florence. The numerous travel books written and illustrated by him include *Road-Book from London to Naples* of 1835 and *Italy, Classical, Historical and Picturesque*, London 1842-44.

*Theodor Mommsen (1817-1903)*
German historian and philologist, famous above all for the *Romische Geschichte*, he travelled to Italy in 1844-45 and following this experience, wrote his *Italienische Reise*.

*Frederic Bourgeois De Mercey (1808-1871)*
He was a good landscape painter. In 1840, he joined the French Ministry for the Interior, and became Director of the Arts, having discontinued painting due to a weakening of his eyesight. Amongst his works, are *Le Tyrol et le nord de l'Italie, esquisses et moeurs*, Paris, 1833, *Les Alpes francaises e le haute Italie*, Paris, 1857, and *La Toscane e le Midi de l'Italie*, Paris, 1858.

*John William De Forest (1826-1906)*
American writer, born in Seymour (Conn.) and died in New Haven. He travelled in Italy, staying some months in Florence. Considered by W.D. Howells and E. Wilson to be the first realist novelist. His Florentine stay inspired *European Acquaintance*, London, 1858.

*Thomas Adolphus Trollope (18?-1892)*
English writer, historian and journalist. T.A. Trollope was the author of numerous books on travel and one of the first to propose, after the Unity of Italy in 1861, itineraries different from those traditionally linked to the eighteenth century *Grand Tour* in *A Lenten Journey in Umbria and the Marches*, London, 1862.

*John Addington Symonds (1840-1893)*
English writer and art historian. His long journies through Italy inspired two volumes, of *The Renaissance in Italy*, London, 1875-1886. The passage dedicated to Piero della Francesca is taken from the volume, *The Fine Arts*, London, 1875, part of the above mentioned series. Together with Walter Pater, his works contributed to the birth of the aesthetic movement. Symonds was the author of biographies and the translator of the sonnets of Michelangelo and of Campanella.

*William Davies (1813-1873)*
English pre-raphaelite painter and writer, Davies explored the Tiber from the estuary to its source. He narrated his journey, mainly undertaken on mule or on foot, in the pleasant volume, *the Pilgrimage of the Tiber from its Source*, London 1873. He was accompanied by the famous American artist, Elihu Vedder. Davies was responsible for detailed descriptions of minor places, almost always neglected by travellers, including the castello Bufalini at San Giustino Umbro and the mountain village of Val Savignone.

*Egerton Ryerson Williams Jr. (1873-1925)*
American lawyer and writer, son of Egerton Ryerson and Ella Louise Hayden. Having been educated at St. Paul's School in Concord, N.H. he graduated in law at Yale University. He practiced the legal profession in Rochester. From 1903, he lived in Italy, in Naples, with Turner and Co. In 1904, Houghton Mifflin of Boston published his *Hill Towns of Italy*. He was the most sensitive and attentive amongst those who described the more famous monuments and the more secluded corners of Sansepolcro.

*Maurice Hewlett (1861-1923)*
English poet, author and essayist. Hewlett's long and impassioned sojourn in Italy can be easily reconstructed from his *Letters*, London, 1926, from which it appears that he visited Venice, Verona, Padua and Ferrara in 1898 and the following year, Mantua. Padua, in particular, also appears in his novels, such as *Ippolita in the Hills*

in the publication, *Little Novels of Italy*, London 1899. His masterpiece, however, is *The Road to Tuscany. A Commentary.* New York, 1904, the result of an extended excursion including the minor cities and the tiniest villages of the region between March and May of 1902.

*Henry James (1843-1916)*
American writer who lived in Europe almost all his life. Many of his novels are set in Italy, in Venice, Florence or Rome and outline the theme of the past's ability to take possession. In love with Italy, James stayed there often in 1872 -1873, in 1892 and at the beginning of the century. *Italian Hours* was published in Boston, New York and London, in 1909, having previously appeared in newspapers and magazines.

*Edward Hutton (1875-1969)*
British author in love with Italian art and literature, to which he dedicated almost forty volumes. A great traveller and divulgator, he commenced with writings dedicated to cities and regions of Italy, amongst which *The Cities of Umbria* 1905 and *Siena and the Southern Tuscany*, London, 1910. Hutton lived in Settignano and was amongst the founders of the British Institute of Florence, where he worked from 1918 to 1954.

*Paul G. Konody (1872-1933)*
English journalist and art critic, working with the "Observer" and the "Daily Mail",

126   he described his travels through Italy by car, a *White Steam* with 30 horse power, in the delightful book, *Through the Alps and the Appennines*, London, Kegan Paul, 1911. He was accompanied by four friends linked by their love of Italy, with whom he experiments totally new roads, in the history of tourism in Italy. The descriptions of the halts, to snatch photographs or sketches, but also to fill up the water of the radiator or discover unfindable petrol pumps, are extremely amusing. Konody described the Resurrection by Piero in Sansepulcro in the volume compiled by R. Wilenski, *Italian Painting*, London.

*Aldous Huxley (1894-1963)*
Famous English author of *Crome Yellow*, 1921, *Point counter Point*, 1928, and *Brave New World*, 1932. He was an untiring traveller and author of diverse volumes of notes and reflections on travel. The text of *Along the Road, Notes and Essays of a Tourist*, London 1924 is mostly dedicated to Italy. The beautiful essay on Piero della Francesca, *The Best Picture*, is taken from this book.

*Andre Maurel (1863-1943)*
French writer. After intense activity as a journalist and novelist, he achieved great success with his travel books on Italy: *Petites villes d'Italie*, consisting of four series published between 1906 and 1911; *Paysages d'Italie*, published between 1912 and 1920 ( the extract on Piero della Francesca is taken from the volume *De Milan a Rome*, Paris, 1913); and *L'art de voyager en Italie*, 1920, and many others.

*Andre Suarès (1868-1948)*
Pseudonym of Félix-André-Yves Scantrel, French essayist of aesthetic taste.
After Stendhal, Suarès is perhaps the most sophisticated interpreter of Italian artistic topography. This relationship unfolds through five journey, from 1895 to 1928, and is transcribed into three books, entitled *Voyage du condottière*. The third volume, *Sienne la bien aimée*, Paris 1932, contains the notes on Sansepolcro and Piero.

*Bernard Berenson (1865-1959)*
American art historian of Lithuanian origin. After studying at Harvard, he travelled through various European countries before establishing himself in Florence, where he bought the villa "I Tatti". He dedicated much of his time to the attribution and archaeology of mediaeval and renaissance Italian art. It was this activity which allowed him to construct the notable collection today conserved at "I Tatti". *The Italian Painters of the Renaissance*, published in Oxford in 1932 in its definitive edition and translated by E. Cecchi in 1954 into Italian, contains some of his most important studies. The studies on Piero appeared in a definitive collection in 1950. The most significant works are *Method and Attribution* of 1947 and the autobiography, *Echoes and Reflections*, Milan, 1949.

*Kenneth Clark (1903-?)*
English art historian and fine essayist, Clark was Director of the Ashmolean Museum in Oxford and the National Gallery of London. He was Professor in History of Art at the University of Oxford and then President of the Arts Council of Great Britain. His studies range from the lively and pleasant *Gothic Revival*, London, 1928, to essay works such as *Landscape into Art*, London, 1949. For British television he directed and commentated the exemplary artistic documentary "Civilization".

# Chronology of his life and works

**circa 1420**
Piero was born in Borgo San Sepolcro around 1420, son of Benedetto di Pietro dei Franceschi, a merchant of leathers, and later wools, and of Romana from the nearby village of Monterchi.

**1439-1440**
Piero is mentioned as an associate or assistant of Domenico Veneziano in the payment of frescoes for the Cappella Maggiore of S. Egidio, Florence, which are now lost. In the same year he was present at the opening of the Council for the Union of the Christian Church from the East and the West and at the arrival of Giovanni VIII Paleologo, Emperor of the East, to Florence. Work in the church of S. Egidio continued throughout 1440.

**1441**
Borgo San Sepolcro fell under Florentine dominion.

**1442**
Piero appeared amongst those eligible for the Borough Council of San Sepolcro. This implies that he held a good social position and was on reasonable terms with the Florentine political administration.

**1445**
Signing of the laborious contract for the polyptych of the Compagnia della Misericordia representing the *Madonna della Misericordia*, the execution of which lasted for many years. The *Baptism of Christ*, considered by many to be a youthful work, was painted by Piero for the Badia and is today in the National Gallery of London. This painting has been dated between 1440 and 1450, but some believe it to be later, between 1460-1462.

**1449-1451**
Correspondence between Giovanni de' Medici and Sigismondo Pandolfo Malatesta contains a possible reference to Piero concerning the frescoes for the Tempio Malatestiano. In 1450 Piero painted a *Penitent St. Jerome*, now in the Museum of Berlin, as well as the *St. Jerome with a donor*, now in the Galleria dell'Accademia in Venice. The following year he finished the fresco for the Tempio Malatestiano in Rimini of *S. Sigismondo with Sigismondo Pandolfo Malatesta*. In about 1450 Piero was in Ferrara to execute a series of paintings for the Castle of the Estensi, of which no trace remains. He had his first link with the Montefeltro di Urbino. Through Ferrara and Urbino, he came into contact with Flemish painting.

**1452-1466**
It was during this considerable length of time that the main chapel of S. Francesco in Arezzo was frescoed with stories from the *Legend of the True Cross*. The initial date is certain, since Piero substituted Bicci di Lorenzo, who died during the course of that year. It is also certain

that the frescoes were completed by 1466. Some critics date the frescoes of S. Francesco to the years 1452-1458, previous to Piero's journey to Rome. Others believe the work was concluded after his stay in Rome.

**1453-1454**
Piero was in San Sepolcro, where he took part in a military parade. The Compagnia della Misericordia lamented the delay in the delivery of the polyptych. Piero was commissioned to execute the *Polyptych for the Church of S. Agostino*. The fact that the artist requested eight years for its completion suggests more important, simultaneous commitments outside his home town. The central part of the à *Polytypch of St. Augustine*, executed after 1460, has been lost. The lateral partitions and a scene from the predella are now in Italian and foreign museums.

**1455-1460**
The frescoes painted by Piero for his native town date to these years: the *Madonna del Parto* in the chapel of the cemetry of Monterchi, the *Resurrection* in the Civic Museum, previously the Palazzo dei Conservatori di San Sepolcro, and the *St. Julian*, also in the Civic Museum. In 1458 Piero named his elder brother, Marco, as his attorney in view of his lengthy absence from San Sepolcro. The following year payment was registered for frescoes by Piero in rooms of the Vatican in Rome. These were probably destroyed in a fire during the same year.

**1460-1470**
Piero designed the S. Ludovico in honour of Ludovico Acciaioli in 1460, which was perhaps executed by his assistants. His name is present among the members of the Collegio dei Probiviri di San Sepolcro. Various works are dated to this period: the *Magdalene* in the Cathedral of Arezzo; the *Hercules* in the family house in San Sepolcro, now in the collection of Isabella Stewart Gardner in Boston; the so-called *Polyptych of Perugia*, painted by Piero for the Convent of the Monache di S. Antonio in Perugia and now in the Galleria Nazionale dell'Umbria. In 1466 Piero was in Arezzo, where the local Compagnia dell'Annunziata, having seen the completed main chapel of S. Francesco, commissioned a standard, now lost. In 1469 he was in Urbino as guest of Giovanni Santi, father of Raphael, to examine the altar-piece painted by Paolo Uccello for the Compagnia del Corpus Domini. Evidence of these profitable years in Urbino can be found in the enigmatic *Flagellation*, painted for the Court of Montefeltro, and in the *Madonna di Senigallia*, executed for the Church of S. Maria delle Grazie fuori le mura in Senigallia. Both these works are now in the Galleria Nazionale delle Marche in Urbino.

**1472-1475**
A series of public acts document Piero's fairly

# Itineraries

continuous presence in San Sepolcro. He painted some panels, now lost. The unfinished *Nativity* in the National Gallery of London perhaps can be dated to these years. In Urbino he completed the great *Altar-piece with the Virgin, Child, Saints and Federico da Montefeltro in prayer* for the Church of S. Bernardino, now in the Gallery of the Brera in Milan. He painted the two portraits of *Federico da Montefeltro and of Battista Sforza*, with the *Triumphs* on the reverse, now in the Uffizi, Florence.

**1478-1486**

Piero made repeated visits to Urbino. He wrote the treatise *De Prospectiva pingendi*. He dedicated his second treatise, *Libellus de quinque corporibus regolaribus*, to Guidobaldo, son of Federico da Montefeltro. His fellow countryman, Luca Pacioli, transcribed most of this in his *De divina proportone*. In 1482 Piero rented a house in Rimini in order to execute a painting.

**1487**

Piero's testament was drawn up, in which he requested to be buried with his family in the badia, now the Cathedral.

**1492**

Piero died on 12th October. The death certificate registers his burial "in badia".

**A Pilgrimage to Piero**
By way of an introduction
Following ancient routes
Piero della Francesca landscapes
A journey through time

**The Florentine Itinerary**
The early Florentine Renaissance
Florence, or the view
Echoes of foreign travellers, from Moryson to Henry James
Piero in Florence: the diptych of the Duke and Duchess of Urbino
the triumphs and their landscapes
The apprenticeship of Piero: an itinerary
Domenico Veneziano
Beato Angelico
Masaccio
Masolino da Panicale
Paolo Uccello
The International Gothic
The Flemish painters
Other contacts, influences and directions

*City Itinerary*
Gallery of the Uffizi
Bargello
Baptistry of S. Giovanni
S. Maria del Fiore and Giotto's Bell-Tower
Piazza SS. Annunziata
Convent of S. Marco
Cenacolo of S. Apollonia
S. Maria Novella
S. Maria del Carmine
S. Croce and the Chapel of the Pazzi

**Florence to Arezzo**
Following a part of the Grand Tour
Historic inns
The Road to Ancona
Aretine valleys

*Itinerary*
Motorway A 1, toll station Firenze Sud
FFSS Station, S. Maria Novella
Ordinary road : SS 67 to Pontassieve and then SS 69 Valdarno along the ancient road to Incisa,
Figline, S. Giovanni, Montevarchi

**Arezzo, the cycle of the 'Legend of the Cross'**
Views of the city
Echoes of Famous travellers
The first encounter with Piero: the Magdalene
S. Francesco in the nineteenth century: an inaccessible church.
The first visitors
Arezzo in Piero's day
The Legend of the Cross

# Bibliography

130    The publictions listed below refer mainly to travellers and admirers of Piero della Francesca, his works and his native land, but includes the main works of criticism on the artist.

Plinio il Giovane, (V. 6 *A Domizio Apollinaire, Epistulae*, 109 d.C.).

G. Vasari, *Le vite*, Firenze, 1550.

M.E. de Montaigne, Il *Journal de voyage en Italie*, written in 1580-1581, it was only published in 1774.

D. Lambardi, *Cronaca del viaggio di Cosimo II dei Medici a Borgo San Sepolcro*, 1612, in M. Betti e G. Tricca, *Il Palio della balestra a Sansepolcro*, Firenze, 1985.

F. Moryson, *Itinerary Containing His Ten Years Travels*, London, 1617.

J. Furttenbach, *Newes Itinerarium Italiae*, Ulm, 1627.

Henri II de Bourbon, *Voyage de M. le Prince de Condé en Italie*, Paris, 1666.

J. Ray, *Travels through Low-Countries, Germany, Italy and France*, London, 1673.

Anonimo, *Cronaca di pellegrinaggio a Loreto*, XVII sec., in A. Brilli, *Borgo San Sepolcro. Viaggio nella città di Piero*, Città di Castello, 1988.

Anonimo, *Guida di Pellegrinaggio a Loreto*, XVII sec., in A. Brilli, *Op. cit.*

T. Smollett, *Travels through France and Italy*, London, 1766.

W. Goethe, *Italienische Reise*, Tubingen, 1829.

S. Rogers, *Italian Journal*, Oxford, 1814.

Stendhal, *Rome, Naples, Florence*, Paris, 1817.

Lady Morgan, *Italy*, London, 1821.

W. Brockedon, *Road-book from London to Naples*, London, 1835.
*Guida d'Italia*, Milano, 1840.

T. Mommsen, *Tagebuch der französich-italienischen Reisen*, 1844-1845.

W.B. Spence, *The Lions of Florence*, 1849.

J. Dennistoun, *Memoirs of the Dukes of Urbino*, London, 1851.

J.W. De Forest, *European Acquaintance*, London, 1858.

F.B. De Mercey, *La Toscana et le Midi dell'Italie*, Paris, 1858.

*Viaggio in Italia. Nuovissima Guida*, Milano, 1861.

T.A. Trollope, *A Lenten Journey in Umbria and the Marches*, London, 1862.

L. Simonin, *L'Etrurie et les Etrusques. Souvenirs de Voyage*, Bruxelles, 1866.

W. Davies, *The Pilgrimage of the Tiber from its Source*, London, 1873.

J.C. Robinson, *«The Times»* (on the acquisition of the *Baptism* by Piero and the *Nativity*) 15 June 1874.

J.A. Symonds, *The Renaissance in Italy. The Fine Arts*, 1875.

A.J. Cuthbert Hare, *Cities of Central Italy*, London, 1876.

E. Müntz, *Florence et la Toscane*, Paris, 1890.

E.R. Williams jr., *Hill Towns of Italy*, Boston, 1904.

M. Hewlett, *The Roads in Tuscany*, London, 1904.

H. James, *Italian Hours*, Boston, 1909.

E. Hutton, *Siena and the Southern Tuscany*, London, 1910.

O.M. Potter, *A Little Pilgrimage in Italy*, London, 1911.

P.G. Konody, *Through the Alps and the Appennines*, London, 1911.

A. Maurel, *Paysages d'Italie*, Paris, 1913.

O. Braun, *Diari, 1908-1918*, Bari, 1923 (*Tagebuch, 1908-1918*).

A. Huxley, *Along the Road. Notes and Essays of a Tourist*, London, 1924.

R. Longhi, *Piero della Francesca*, Roma, 1927.

A. Suarès, *Voyage du Condottière*, Paris, 1932.

M. Denis, *Charmes et Leçons de l'Italie*, Paris, 1933.

A. Camus, *Noches*, Paris, 1939.

A. Camus, Diari inediti cit. in F. Di Pilla, *A. Camus e la città del dialogo*, Perugia, 1988.

G.M. Trevelyan, *Garibaldi's Defence of the Roman Republic*, London, 1935.

M. Salmi, *La pittura di Piero della Francesca*, Bergamo, 1940 (poi Novara, 1979).

K. Clark, *Landscape into Art*, London, 1949.

K. Clark, *Piero della Francesca*, Venezia, 1970 (*Piero della Francesca*, 1951).

B. Berenson, *I Pittori italiani del Rinascimento*, Firenze, 1954 (*Italian Painters of the Renaissance*, Electa, 1894-1907).

B. Berenson, *Piero della Francesca or the Ineloquent in Art*, London, 1954.

H.V. Morton, *A Traveller in Italy*, London, 1957.

D. Formaggio, *Piero della Francesca*, Milano, 1957.

C. Rosini, *Città di Castello. Guida estetica*, Città di Castello, 1961.

L. Berti, *Il Museo di Arezzo*, I, Roma, 1961.

L.L. Notestein, *Hill Towns of Italy*, London, 1963.

C. Gilbert, *Change in Piero della Francesca*, Locus Valley, N.Y. 1968.

M. Rowdon, *The Companion Guide to Umbria*, London, 1969.

G. Marchini, *L'architettura nell'aretino*, in AA.VV. *L'architettura nell'aretino: il primo Rinascimento*, Roma, 1969.

M. Salmi, *Civiltà artistica della terra aretina*, Novara, 1971.

E. Battisti, *Piero della Francesca*, Milano, 1971.

L. Gardiner, *Un fiume lontano da Roma*, in *Onoranze a Michelangelo*, Cortona, 1971.

A. Brilli, *Borgo San Sepolcro. Guida turistica*, San Sepolcro, 1972.

K. Clark, *The Other Half. A Self Portrait*, London, 1977.

R. Guttuso, *Come sento Piero della Francesca* in «Nuova Antologia», fasc. 2110, ottobre 1976, pp. 171 e sgg.

A. Tafi, *Immagine di Arezzo*, Arezzo, 1978.

C. Ginzburg, *Indagini su Piero*, Torino, 1981.

M. Martelli, F. Nibbi, *Arezzo. Guida storica e artistica*, Arezzo, 1982.

W. Weaver, *Wintering in Tuscany. Exploring Arezzo, an Italian Hill Town*, in «The New York Times», 16 Dec. 1984.

O. Calabrese a cura di, *Piero teorico dell'arte*, saggi di H. Damish, D. Arasse, A. Parronchi, L. Marin, G. Arrighi, M. Apa, J. Petitot, T. Martone, G. Pittaluga, E. Battisti, Roma, 1985.

A. Marshall Zwack, *Florence the Magnificent*, in «Travel and Leisure», April 1987.

S. Hall, *Heading for the Hill Towns*, in «Travel and Leisure», April, 1987.

J. Mortimer, *Summer's Lease*, Harmondsworth, 1988.

A. Brilli, *Borgo San Sepolcro. Viaggio nella città di Piero*, Città di Castello, 1988.

A.M. Maetzke, D. Galoppi Nappini, *Il Museo civico di Sansepolcro*, Firenze, 1988.

AA.VV., *Un Progetto per Piero della Francesca*, Firenze, 1989.

A. Paolucci, *Piero della Francesca*, Firenze, 1989.

Stampato per conto di Electa
dalla Fantonigrafica di Venezia